Careers in the
Film Industry

Careers in the
Film Industry

Ricki Ostrov

**Kogan
Page**

First published 1984 by Kogan Page Ltd
120 Pentonville Road, London N1 9JN

Copyright © Kogan Page Ltd 1984

British Library Cataloguing in Publication Data
Ostrov, Ricki
    Careers in the film industry.— (Kogan Page
    careers series)
    1. Moving-picture industry — Great Britain —
    Vocational guidance
    I. Title
    384'.8'0941   PN1993.5.G7

    ISBN 0-85038-723-X (Hb)
    ISBN 0-85038-724-8 (Pb)

Printed and bound in Great Britain by
The Camelot Press Ltd, Southampton

Contents

Introduction

Early Days

The first motion pictures made were two-dimensional, black and white, and very short — one or two minutes at most. They were shown on a kinetoscope, developed by the American inventor Thomas Edison, in 1889, who opened his first public kinetoscope parlour on Broadway in April 1894. The viewer looked through a peephole into a darkened cabinet and turned a spool. The 50-foot film ran for less than a minute. The first films shown on the kinetoscope were factual: a baby being bathed, a dog with a bone, an erotic dance and a boxing match.

The basic principles of the cinema had been known for centuries. The *camera obscura* had been invented in Italy in the sixteenth century, and the magic lantern had been first described by the Jesuit, Athanasius Kircher, in 1646. What made the leap from these Renaissance toys to the cinema were the invention of photography by Fox Talbot, and the observation by Peter Mark Roget of Roget's *Thesaurus*, while looking through a Venetian blind, that movement could be broken down into a series of separate phases — both in the early nineteenth century.

At the same time that Edison was developing his kinetoscope, a Frenchman, Emile Reynaud, was working on what he called his praxinoscope, based on hand-drawn images projected on to a screen, making him the father of animation. Edison's 'peepshow' used photography but not projection. Reynaud's praxinoscope used projection but not photography. The two concepts were brought together by another Frenchman, Louis Lumière, who staged the world's first film projection at the Grand Café in Boulevard des Capucines in Paris on 28 December 1895. The following year, 1896, saw the first kiss on the screen, a 15-second extract from the popular play, *The Widow Jones*, starring Mary Irwin and John C Rice. The motion picture industry was born.

That same year saw the first public cinema showing in England, at the Marlborough Hall in Regent Street on 20 February 1896, by yet another Frenchman, Félicien Trewey, a conjuror by profession. In June, the Prince of Wales visited the Alhambra Theatre and watched his own horse, Persimmon, win the Derby. It was the British film industry's first Royal Command Performance.

The cinema mushroomed but the films that were made remained documentaries. Motion picture cameras covered the Oxford and Cambridge Boat Race, the Boer War and Queen Victoria's funeral. With the new century, storylines and fiction films made their first appearance. In 1902 Méliés made his famous *Trip to the Moon*, the world's first science fiction film, and in 1903 Edison filmed *The Great Train Robbery*, the first Western. Inevitably, the first popular fictitious film made in England was about an animal, *Rescued by Rover* (1905).

George Pearson, Britain's first major film producer, described this embryo cinema in his autobiography: 'Suddenly things happened, someone turned down a gas-jet, the tin apparatus burst into a fearful clatter, and an oblong picture slapped on to the screen and began a violent dance. After a while I discerned it was a picture of a house, but a house on fire. Flames and smoke belched from the windows, and the miracle of miracles, a fire-engine dashed in, someone mounted a fire escape, little human figures darted about below and then . . . Bang! . . . the show was over. Exactly one minute . . . I had been to the cinema.'

Film-makers had always sought to add colour to film and, in the spring of 1896, hand-coloured films were exhibited. The process was tedious and time consuming. Many different techniques were tried to add colour, including stencils, chemical toning and dyes, but none could satisfactorily reproduce the original colour. A two-colour system, the kinemacolor process, was developed in 1906 and stayed popular for over ten years. The first technicolour film, *The Toll of the Sea*, was shown in 1922 and was a big step forward. By the end of the 1920s many films, including *Broadway Melody of 1929*, were in colour.

In the early 1900s most movies were still exhibited in fairgrounds and were basically one-man operations. Producers devised their own equipment, their families acted and they distributed and sold their own films. By the second decade of cinema's existence, however, there was a tremendous change. Feature length films which had a distinct, narrative structure were being made. An entire industry was being established around the making of movies. A hierarchy developed. with producers, directors and actors having separate and clearly defined responsibilities. The cost of production increased enormously. Studios were being constructed in and around London and Hollywood dominated the motion picture industry.

The Talkies

It took movies over 30 years to learn to speak. Edison was unsuccessful at matching sound to picture in his original machines. Most movies were shown with some sort of musical accompaniment, from a lone piano player to a full orchestra. After the turn of the century most feature films had musical scores specially composed for them. Music, however, was not the only sound that accompanied these early movies. Some cinemas were equipped with special machines that provided sound effects, ranging from the sound of horses galloping and birds singing to the sound of gunfire. The films of D W Griffith, such as *Birth of a Nation*, had elaborate musical scores which were obviously more successful in larger cinemas with proper facilities than small town movie houses.

It was clear that satisfactory sound accompaniment had to be recorded and reproduced mechanically. By the early

1920s, some of the problems were overcome. But the most pressing problem was making certain that sound and image fitted perfectly. The first systems had the sound recorded on a separate disc and then synched up, but to synch it perfectly the sound was needed on the same strip of film. Experiments proved that sound waves could be converted into electrical impulses and then registered on the celluloid itself; this would become the sound track, the narrow band running down the edge of the film and printed directly on it.

At this time large film companies were not interested in talking movies and were more concerned about the threat of radio. Warner Bros was the first big studio to take the risk with sound. They built their own sound stages and, working with Western Electric, were able to produce their own sound pictures. They were still using the sound on disc method rather than trying to fit sound on to film. *Don Juan*, starring John Barrymore and Mary Astor, was the first film premiered with a fully synchronised score. Audiences were more interested in musical accompaniment and not necessarily talking pictures. The movie was highly successful and ran for over six months. But it was *The Jazz Singer*, with Al Jolson, that assured the domination of American films in the talkie era. It premiered on 9 October 1927 and although movies already talked and sang, something about this film captured the imagination of the audience and the rush was on. Most film companies now investigated and researched sound for film and agreed to perfect the sound on film method, rather than sound on disc which was what Warner Bros used. In 1928 nearly 80 feature length films with sound were made. The silent film was now dated and archaic. Warner Bros released the first all-talkie, *Lights of New York*, which, although not a very good film, was a huge success. Fox, MGM, Paramount, Universal and RKO all had talkies out in that year. Walt Disney also produced a talking animated cartoon in 1928, *Steamboat Willie*; it starred a mouse called Mickey.

By the end of 1928 every significant American studio

had talking pictures in release. Cinema attendance had been falling and sound came at a good time. There was a renewal of interest in the movies with the addition of this novelty and box office receipts increased about 50 per cent with the introduction of sound. The film industry rode out the crash of 1929 — much of this being due to the experimentation and addition of sound to picture.

Sound also changed the nature of film production drastically. New sound stages had to be built at all the studios. New technology — silent cameras, microphones on booms — had to be developed. The careers of many well known silent film starts, such as John Gilbert, were ruined when it was found that their voices were not acceptable on film. The comedians were the hardest hit. Buster Keaton and Harry Langdon were just two of the casualties. Audiences also became more discerning. They wanted stories along with sound. Sound films survived their original novelty value and became acclaimed in their own right.

With the depression, the bonanza that followed the start of sound had evaporated by 1931. Hollywood was desperate and was borrowing heavily from banks. Film companies could no longer count on profits to plough back into production. By 1933, box office receipts were way down and film companies depended on certain types of movies to assure financial success. Although there was little money around, audiences still seemed to find it to go to the movies; they wanted dreams in cinemas to escape the poverty in real life. So films acquired a new dimension with sound and large scale, lavish musicals benefited greatly. Busby Berkeley, the master of spectacle, had movies out like *42nd Street*, *Footlight Parade* and probably his best known, *Gold Diggers of 1933*. RKO had an unbeatable team with Fred Astaire and Ginger Rogers, who danced their way into the hearts of millions. Horror movies, such as *King Kong*, *Dracula* and *Frankenstein* helped audiences escape from the harsh realities they faced. The 1930s was also the richest decade for comedies, as laughter was another antidote to the depression. Audiences wanted to have something to laugh at.

The Influence of Hollywood

The British film industry was used to growing up in the shadow of Hollywood and talkies ensured the dominance of American films. By 1929, Hollywood was turning out talkies faster than Britain could accommodate, but by the end of 1930 all main British studios had converted to sound production. British films had broad appeal ranging from comedies to harshly realistic documentaries, but it was difficult getting them shown on home territory. The major Hollywood companies still had a lot of control in Britain. They produced films in this country for the English market, and Warner Bros even set up an American production company in England.

In 1927 the Cinematograph Films Act (Quota Act) was passed, which established a quota for the number of British films that had to be shown. Its aim was to ensure the distribution and exhibition of British-made features, providing a stimulus to production. Many British distributors were merely branches of major Hollywood studios and handling the home product was not a priority, just a routine. The studios scheduled their own films far in advance of release and packaged less popular American films with the more prestigious. Instead of encouraging the production of quality British films, the quota was filled by quick, cheaply-made films that were rushed out.

Possibly because of the dominance of Hollywood and the artificial protectionism of the Quota Act, British film-makers made little effort to compete with American feature films. Instead, Britain developed another form of film art, the documentary. Established from simple and mundane beginnings to promote trade and economic co-operation with the British Empire, the documentary of the 1930s became Britain's greatest contribution to the cinema in the inter-war years, and the parent of television realism. The guiding light behind the British documentary movement was John Grierson, who although he visited Hollywood in the 1920s, and wrote perceptively about fiction films in the 1930s, was never interested in film as entertainment. He drew his inspiration from the socialist realism of Eisenstein and the romantic naturalism of Robert Flaherty. Nor were the majority of those who worked with Grierson interested in film as entertainment. They were upper middle class, Cambridge-educated, radical and idealist. Hollywood was enemy territory.

As Grierson himself wrote: 'In the beginning we set out to use the film to report on what we saw, and to report on the world in which we lived. It was in a period of growing social consciousness — it was during the early period, the great wave of social democracy, and we almost inevitably associated development of the documentary film with the progress of the working class, the developments in science and technology, the growth of international relationships of one kind and another, and the social problems thrown up in our modern surroundings.'

The central figure in these documentaries — *Drifters*, *Man of Aran*, *Coalface* and *Industrial Britain* — was man, man struggling against nature, and discovering his dignity in that struggle. Thanks to Grierson the real world was opened up to the cinema. As he said, 'The raw can be finer (more real in the philosophic sense) than the acted article. Spontaneous gesture has a special value on the screen.'

But documentaries were hardly entertainment, and in the world of entertainment British films were still suburban compared to Hollywood. Already by the mid-1930s it was obvious that the quota did not create a flourishing entertainment industry. There was a migration of talent to Hollywood, which paid higher salaries, had bigger production budgets and better working conditions, but at the same time, talented European refugees were coming to Britain, adding quality to British films. During the second half of that decade, the film industry was hit by a major depression. Britain could not compete with American companies which began buying up bankrupt studios and filming in Britain. The City was not providing finance, studios were in trouble and there was a much needed injection of cash when Americans arrived to film. Twentieth Century-Fox and Henry Fonda came to Britain in 1936 and produced the first technicolour film in this country, *Wings of a Morning*. Although the backing was American, the film brought much needed work and experience in colour photography to Britain. In 1937 Robert Taylor filmed *A Yank at Oxford* for MGM which provided another injection of cash into the floundering British industry.

Then a government committee, under Lord Moyne, repealed the quota. By the end of the 1930s cinema attendance was booming again, mostly due to the American product. Distribution and exhibition were extremely profitable, but film production was still depressed. British films just could not compete, either here or in America. The quota was reinstated, but films now had to meet certain minimum production costs. This effectively killed off the 'quickie quota' film. Many of the films produced involved American studios at some stage and they now began serious production in Britain.

The British Film Industry

The outbreak of World War II almost killed the British motion picture industry. Cinemas were closed and studios were commandeered. Following pressure by the British film industry cinemas quickly re-opened. 'The public has always wanted good British films,' Sidney Bernstein, head of Granada, appealed, 'not the million-pound "epics" which so often bore them, but the good honest unpretentious stories in which we have shown such promise . . . the records of everyday English life.' Alas, the early British war films hardly justified the re-opening of the cinemas, and films like Alexander Korda's *The Lion Has Wings* were as boring as they were uplifting. Only in documentaries did film rise to the occasion. Documentary metamorphosed itself into propaganda and propaganda metamorphosed itself into art. In the hands of Grierson and his protégées, cinema became a major weapon, with films like Pat Jackson's *Western Approaches*, Humphrey Jennings's *Fires Were Started* and Harry Watts's *Target for Tonight.* There was nothing crude, preaching or heavy-handed about them. They were harsh and realistic, concerned less with ideas than with ordinary people, and ordinary people flocked to see them. 2,240,000 went to see Crown Film Unit documentaries in 1940; by 1944 this figure had swollen to 6,500,000.

The early war documentaries were made on a shoe-string, like Humphrey Jennings's *Fires Were Started* which used amateurs (the novelist William Sansom playing Barrett, the new fireman). They were cheaply-made, hard-hitting and, in terms of ideology, highly unofficial and often disapproved of by the powers that be. By the middle of the War the government's attitude had changed. Vast budgets were imposed, big-name scriptwriters like Terence Rattigan and E M Forster were conscripted and professional actors began to make their appearance. In the films that emerged — *Desert Victory*, *Tunisian Victory* and *Burma Victory* — there was a loss of quality. The ultimate of the documentary block-busters, *The True Glory*, an 'official' record of the War, which used a total of six and a half million feet of film and was narrated in pretentious blank verse, had all the pomp of an Elgar symphony.

The early war documentaries did, however, have a profound effect on conventional British cinema — after its embarrassing start with *The Lion Has Wings*. A beginning had already been made in 1940 with the release of two British films, *Proud Valley* (the story of a negro, Paul Robeson, who moves into a Welsh mining village, is first rejected and then accepted, and dies saving the life of the son of the man who first befriended him) and *Love on the Dole* (which can be compared to George Orwell's *Down and Out in Paris and London*). As unexpected box-office successes, they showed that there was an intelligent and discerning audience hungry for more than just 'quota quickies' or histrionic histories of Queen Elizabeth I. A whole genre of films merging documentary and drama — *In Which We Serve*, *The Way Ahead* and *One of Our Aircraft Is Missing* — grew up. But the greatest of all war-time films had nothing to do with the War: Laurence

Olivier's adaptation of Shakespeare's *Henry V*. Yet, in spite of the scope and the relevance of these films, the standard comedies of Will Hay and George Formby probably did more to keep up British spirits than all the Griersons, Robesons and Oliviers put together.

With the end of World War II, the new cinema talents that had come up through the war years collected at Ealing Studios. There they produced a series of great English comedies — *Passport to Pimlico*, *Hue and Cry*, *Kind Hearts and Coronets, Whisky Galore* and *The Titfield Thunderbolt*. They were the most English of English films, combining comedy and realism, the banal and the ridiculous.

Ealing had fully equipped studios by 1931 and had been set up by Basil Dean. The company was known as Associated Talking Pictures. Dean was the first theatrical personality to promote talking pictures and he tried to encourage other theatrical staff to make the move to the new medium. Directors Carol Reed and Basil Deardon were just two he convinced. In 1938 — the company was then called Ealing — Michael Balcon replaced Dean as the head of production. Ealing had hits with George Formby, and Balcon cultivated a family atmosphere at the studio, encouraging his staff to work as a team. There was a great community spirit and the studio was successful at making English films with English talent. In many ways the Ealing Studios were as 'English' as the Ealing films. Balcon may have prided himself on the family atmosphere but, as Harry Watts who worked there has pointed out, there were three separate hierarchical dining rooms.

There was a considerable difference in the atmosphere at Ealing and the attitude at major American studios. During the 1930s and 1940s, production in America was dominated by a handful of studios. They were involved in production, international distribution and theatre ownership. They had entire stables of talent, from actors and directors down to their own police and medical teams. They looked after their own but expected complete devotion and loyalty in return. They told their players how to act, dress and perform. Although the studios encouraged high standards of excellence, many in the stable wanted to break out on their own. Actors and directors wanted to work independently, and with the threat of television looming, it was cheaper for studios not to have so many employees on contract full time. The studio system began to fall apart. They let many people go, closed some of the stages and also began financing and distributing independent films.

Ealing Studios were sold to the BBC in 1955. Production continued at MGM's Borehamwood Studios and Ealing made its final film in 1959.

The death of Ealing was a sign of the times. Already, by the late 1940s, J Arthur Rank and Hollywood so dominated the British cinema industry that they had a virtual monopoly. A Board of Trade Report — Tendencies to Monopoly in the Cinematograph Film Industry — recommended the nurturing of independent companies as a safeguard against the power of Rank and the Americans. American films were heavily taxed, but rather than safeguard British films it simply provoked the Americans into retaliating against British films with a boycott, while post-war Britain lacked the risk capital to build an independent industry. So pessimistic was the film industry that the main union, ACTT, even advocated nationalisation. So desperate was the situation that the President of the Board of Trade, Harold Wilson, told Parliament: 'Apart from Rank, pretty well the whole of the rest of the industry is now facing a stoppage unless financial provision is made available.'

What saved British films was Harold Wilson's National Film Finance Corporation, set up in 1948 with a government loan of £5 million, and boosted in 1950 with the 'Eady Levy' (named after Sir Wilfred Eady of the Treasury) of a farthing on every ticket sold, and still operating today to provide finance for British film productions. It came just in time. For a new threat to the cinema was appearing: television. In 1950, when there were only 400,000 television licences, 1396 million cinema tickets were sold in 4483 cinemas. By 1959, when there were over nine million television licences, only 600 million cinema tickets were sold in only 3414 cinemas. By 1970, when there were 16 million television licences, only 200 million admissions were made in 1558 cinemas.

The film industry immediately saw television as the enemy, and threatened to boycott any producer who sold his film rights to television. They need not have worried. For television proved a liberation for films, widening the horizons of the cinema, giving the film new dimensions and replacing the captive audience with a discerning one. Rank was the first of the cinema barons to see this and bought up interests in Southern Television, quickly followed by Bernstein's Granada, thus beginning a process that has continued to today, even going into reverse, with Channel 4 becoming one of the main sources of finance for feature films in Britain.

The cinema industry, unable to peer into the future, fought television with family fare and 'cheapies'. Hammer horrors, *Carry On* comedies and complacent war films became the order of the day. The cinema continued its decline until the early 1960s when a 'new wave' of creativity burst on to the screen. *Room At The Top* with Laurence Harvey signalled this change. Profound social and cultural changes had taken place in Britain; it was a time of protest and demonstrations, with the Suez 'moment of truth', anti-nuclear marches and a new affluence and consciousness among teenagers.

At the National Film Theatre, new independent film-makers were showing their work in documentaries. Most dealt with other young, working class people. The film-makers were trying to put a more personal view into film documentaries and rejected studio sets in favour of location shooting, preferably in industrial cities using black and white film and natural lighting. The films were based on books and plays by authors with experience in working class life in the provinces: the Angry Young Men who produced *A Taste of Honey*, *Loneliness of the Long Distance Runner* and *Saturday Night and Sunday Morning* among others.

In 1963 Lindsay Anderson, one of Britain's New Wave, released his first feature film, *This Sporting Life*. In that year over a third of the films generally released dealt with aspects of contemporary life in Britain. But, also in that year *Tom Jones*, financed by the American studio, United Artists, was a huge success. The theme of the movie, being uninhibited and free spirited, caught the mood of the moment. London was swinging and America was ready to cash in. James Bond also made his first appearance then — he was cool, knowing and stylish — characteristic of the 1960s. Britain was by then the music and fashion capital of the world; being British was 'in' and American companies were more than willing to capitalise on this. Many of the New Wave film-makers made features during this period; *Darling*, *Morgan* and *Alfie* showed London life at its best. American companies realised that production costs were lower in Britain and there was a great wealth of untapped talent to utilise.

Many of the same changes that were sweeping Britain were also affecting America during the 1960s. It was a time of social change and revolution, with the new Kennedy administration, the political and social awakening of blacks and women, and the war in Vietnam. Television was also rising in importance and Hollywood began to experiment with new techniques to stem the tide. Many of the key figures of the golden age of Hollywood died or retired and major studios were less and less successful. *Bonnie and Clyde* and *The Graduate* confirmed the birth of a new era. The stars and directors of these new movies were trained in New York theatre rather than Hollywood sound stages. Television replaced Broadway or studio-trained talent as the fund of writers and directors. Television was a medium offering excitement to talented creative young people, especially in that time of dwindling box office receipts and rising production costs.

By the end of the 1960s it was obvious that cinema success depended on the appeal to younger audiences, those with the time, money and energy to go to movies; they formed the bulk of the cinema audiences. Although the new generation may have rejected the dreams and myths of the old Hollywood, there were new dreams to replace them, signified by the success of small, intimate movies such as *Easy Rider* and *The Wild Bunch*. By the end of 1968 almost 90 per cent of the British features were American-financed. The native industry was all but dead. By 1969 however, most Hollywood film companies were heavily in debt and 'Britishness' was *passé*. All-American movies such as *Butch Cassidy* were huge box office smashes and the Hollywood companies pulled out almost as one. There was a recession, unemployment soared, and with the election of a Conservative government, there was a return to the traditional values of the past, both on and off the screen. The British New Wave, long dead, and the success of American-financed British films signalled the change. British cinema had lost most of its native character and became part of the transatlantic movie culture.

It survived on the strength of a few outstanding directors who had come up through the 1960s' New Wave. Few of these directors had gone through the conventional studio system. John Schlesinger, Richard Lester, Ken Russell, Ken Loach and Peter Watkins came up through television. Nicholas Roeg, Hugh Hudson, Ridley Scott and Alan Parker came up through advertising. Some of the films they made, like the films of Garnett and Watkins, were super-realist, others like Roeg's *The Man Who Fell To Earth* had all the slickness of a toothpaste advert, and a few, like Ken Russell's films, were just plain bizarre. What they all had in common was that they appealed to minority audiences which pre-Channel 4 television either could not, or would not, reach. Cinema was no longer a victim of television. It had become an alternative to television.

While cinema in the 1970s was directing itself at minority groups (mostly one group, the young educated middle class who could afford the price of the ticket), Britain's first National Film School was growing up at Beaconsfield in Buckinghamshire. By the mid-1970s the first students to graduate from there — though there were only 25 each year in the early years — were making their first small features and documentaries: Nick Broomfield's and Joan Churchill's *Juvenile Liaison*, Michael Radford's *The White Bird Passes*, Roger Christian's *Black Angel* and Jana Bokova's documentary on Don McCullin. Now, in the 1980s, they have reached their maturity. The films that are now being made: Radford's *Another Time Another Place*, Hugh Herbert's *Chariots of Fire* and Bill Forsyth's *Gregory's Girl* are a sign of that maturity.

With this film renaissance has come a new technical excellence, which has resulted in many American productions, such as *Star Wars*, *Superman III* and the James Bond films, using British studios and cutting rooms for their technical effects. The seeds of this technical excellence can be found in the industry's grounding in advertising and is what director Ridley Scott (who made *Alien*) calls '30-second feature films'.

'As a cinematic training ground for taking short cuts to the quintessential,' wrote American film critic, Harlan Kennedy, about British cinema, 'commercials are without rival: and their influence has rubbed off not just on the men who made them but on all who have "grown up" with them. Neither Peter Greenaway nor the Monty Python team served an apprenticeship in commercials, but like the rest of us they have lived with and learnt from these time-bombs of Instant Drama that explode across our screens each night in a dream-like staccato.' (*Film Comment*, May/June 1980)

The greatest boost for the young film-makers of today has been the arrival of Channel 4. Rather than steal from the cinema the minority market that the cinema had cultivated, it has provided finance for new productions and given producers a new type of deal in which films have six months at the box office before being shown on the screen. As producer David Puttnam put it: 'If a film does well there is a prospect of financial benefits. At the very worst the cost of the cinema exposure can be written off as valuable advance promotion for the film's appearance on TV or its sale to international markets.'

The effect of Channel 4 on British films can be shown

from one glance at the London Film Festival's 1983 programme; of 18 British films, 15 were made with television finance. With Channel 4 has come a new infusion of funds into films via production companies like Rediffusion, UMF, Brittanic, Virgin and Goldcrest. The result is what David Puttnam calls 'a period of renewal in British film production without parallel in the film industry's chequered 70-year-old history'.

Today there are over 10,000 people employed in the film industry, making between 20 and 30 feature films each year, and with the blurring of divisions between film and television, and the growth of video and cable TV, there is hope that the numbers — rather than diminish — may actually increase. 'For the moment,' says Puttnam, 'the appetite of Channel 4 for home-grown films seems like a gift from the gods arriving in a parched land. It has produced a clutch of films, the like of which many of us had lost hope of seeing made in our own language . . . If we can put our own house in order and build on the best of what's left and what's been started, we will see the development of one of the few things we in this country seem to be rather good at — film-making.'

The films of the 1980s emerged from the National Film School, the television training courses and the advertising agencies of the 1970s. The films of the 1990s will emerge from the young people in their teens and twenties who will find a career in film-making in the 1980s. How healthy the British film industry will be then depends on them.

Part 1

Chapter 1
The Structure of the Industry

Organisation

The film industry, located mostly in London, consists mainly of production companies, studios, post-production houses and film distributors.

Production companies, of which there are hundreds around London, actually produce the film. They usually have one or more in-house producers and directors, a secretary or personal assistant, a receptionist and a messenger. The number of permanent staff of most production companies is kept to a minimum, with the technical staff needed for each production being hired on a freelance basis.

The studios, such as Shepperton, Pinewood and Elstree, do not produce films anymore — they do not have permanent film-makers on staff. They are what is known as 'four-walled', letting space and facilities to production companies who usually bring their own crew with them. Some companies are located at the studio full time and others relocate themselves at the studio when they are using the facilities for filming.

The post-production sector of the industry includes the film laboratories and a number of companies providing a variety of services, including editing rooms, film sound recording studios, opticals and special effects.

Film distributors handle the marketing and publicity for films as well as coordinating the physical distribution of film prints to cinemas and screening rooms. Most of the staff is clerical.

Films

We usually think of films as having huge budgets, large, all-star casts and lots of publicity. But there are a number of different types of films, used for a variety of purposes, being made today.

Feature films are those which are specifically intended for cinema release. They are full length, about 110 minutes, and are generally fiction. Because the cost of filming can be high, sometimes running into millions of pounds, there are few British feature films being made. Most of the features shot in Britain are American-financed and produced. Independent productions are usually made on a much smaller budget and are shorter in length. These include movies for both cinema and television viewing and television programmes, including documentaries and shorts.

The making of commercials for television is another area of activity. Although broadcast on television, most commercials are shot on film and then transferred to tape.

There is a wide range of films not intended for commercial or broadcasting purposes. These include government educational and training films, industrial or scientific films and material used for marketing and public relations.

Finance

Raising the money to make a movie can often be the most difficult part of film-making. To begin with, there are a number of government institutions with small sums available for British productions. A complicated cinema tax, called the Eady Levy, provides some of the money available. The British Film Fund Agency administers this money, allocating it to a number of financing organisations, including the National Film Finance Board and the British Film Institute Production Board. Money is also allocated by the Agency to British film-makers who meet certain requirements.

A number of private investment corporations have been set up specifically to raise money to finance films. Until not too long ago, many City investors were reluctant to invest in film-making since it is such a high risk. A change in tax laws and the international success of British films such as *Chariots of Fire* and *Gandhi* have made money-raising a little easier.

There are a number of other methods for raising money, including selling television and foreign distribution rights, guarantees against royalties and deals with American studios and distributors.

Probably the most important source of finance is Channel 4. Though their budget is not the largest, it is consistent and provides a stable funding base, something the industry has been without for a long time. In addition to the monies provided for productions intended for television, Channel 4 also finances British feature films. Often these are shown in cinemas for a specific length of time and are then broadcast on television.

Chapter 2

Working in the Industry

Personal Qualities

If you asked someone in the film industry what quality you needed to succeed, the answer would most often be perseverance. Because of the structure of the industry and the control of the unions, you have to realise that reaching your goal may take years. You need to be willing to continue after many rejections and you have to accept that there may be long periods of unemployment. You need a strong will, a lot of determination, and you need to love what you are doing.

When working on a production, you have to be able to function as a member of a team, to take instructions and directions. You will often have to work long hours, including evenings and weekends, sometimes in bad weather. You need to stay calm under pressure, be creative and open to new ideas and suggestions.

Breaking into the film industry is not easy, no matter how much training you have. There is a lot of competition for jobs and many times when you have finished one job you are immediately out looking for another. You need to be aggressive, adaptable and determined. You have to keep trying — without that determination and perseverance, your chances of succeeding are low.

The Stages of Film-making

There are three steps in film-making, each of them involving different groups of people. Some may be involved in only one stage, some are involved in all three.

Pre-production. This is the stage when all the components are organised in preparation for actual filming. The producer first finds the story or comes up with the concept of the film and he/she will then obtain the financing for the production. During pre-production the director is hired, the film is cast and the crew assembled. Locations and equipment are also provided. A budget and shooting schedule are prepared, and this is often the responsibility of the production manager.

Production. This is the actual filming, or 'shooting' of the picture. It is done either on location or in a studio. A number of jobs, such as assistant director, cameraman, and some sound personnel are actively involved in this stage.

Post-production. The film is processed by a laboratory, edited, and then completed. Editing involves not only cutting the picture, but adding the soundtrack, opticals and special effects. This stage may take longer than the actual filming, especially on feature films or television commercials.

Job Descriptions

The roles and responsibilities of many involved in making a film often overlap and coincide, depending on the type of film being made. Feature films tend to have a much larger crew with several assistants. Documentaries tend to keep the crew down to a minimum. Few technicians have the luxury of working only in one area of film-making — most will do a number of films in one year, including commercials, possibly a feature, and two or three independent productions. Following is a general guide to the jobs available in film-making.

Producer

The producer is the member of the film unit who controls the organisation and finances, and who is the final authority on all practical matters. He/she usually comes up with the idea for the film, obtains the rights to the property if it is a book or script, or oversees the writing of an original screenplay. The producer is also responsible for obtaining the finance. He/she hires the director and is involved in casting, finding locations and hiring the crew. The producer holds the purse strings, making certain that the film can be completed on the amount of money available. The producer puts the entire package together and then monitors the day-to-day progress of the film.

A good producer will be interested in a variety of subjects and is always coming up with new ideas for productions. He/she should be determined, almost totally unreasonable at times and unwilling to take 'no' for an answer. A producer needs to be able to organise more than one job at a time.

Very few producers start out with the intention of producing. Many come from law or business or were originally agents, and a number of producers start their careers as production managers or assistant directors. A producer is the only union grade job for which you do not need a union ticket.

CASE STUDIES
Genny, producer.

> I was a housewife and mother before working in film. My husband is a cameraman, so I knew a lot about the business and most of our friends worked in film.
>
> When my husband set up a production company, I wanted to be involved. I offered to do anything and ended up doing secretarial work and keeping the books. I got more and more involved, helping in different areas and learning how a production actually comes together. I knew how much films cost to make and where the money was spent.
>
> Then a friend asked me to produce a promotional film for him on a tight budget. After that, I made more and more films and eventually set up my own company.
>
> I believe strongly that there is room for more new and creative people in film. I always try and give beginners an opportunity to work on a production. It's important for them to understand what happens on a set and how films are made. If somebody writes to me, and is knowledgeable about what I'm doing, and shows enthusiasm and interest, then

I'll find the time to talk to them. I can't always offer a job, but I can give some advice and help.

Although I didn't realise it, being a housewife gave me a lot of the experience needed by a good producer. When you manage a home, you control and budget the money; you learn how to make it stretch. You have to organise a lot of people and activities and you need to have a lot of patience, something most mothers have in abundance. We also have a sense about other people — when to placate and when to persist. A producer has to be able to get what he/she wants without offending other people.

It isn't difficult to become a producer but there is so little training that makes any sense. Producing is usually more on the management than creative side of film-making.

Being a female producer, you have to be remarkably tough. You're dealing with men and money — two powerful components — and you will need to be aggressive to get what you want.

Sandra, producer.

It's very much a self-motivated industry. Nobody comes to you. If you want to do something in films then you have just got to go out and do it, and you can only do it if you are obsessed. Self-motivation and obsession are the two most important qualities needed. After that comes a belief in yourself and in the people you are working with. And then comes the ability to be able to bluff — to just pick up the phone and ring up anyone, as if you're David Puttnam. And with that — of course — goes that other very important quality: being very thick-skinned.

I came in through the art school system where I did stage design. From there I went to the English National Opera where I did literally anything: running round, helping with the costumes, assisting on the sets, even doing the shopping. After ENO I went to work for a theatrical costumiers, Berners and Nathan, and it was there that I first found myself involved in films, meeting the designers, talking to the actors, getting the costumes out. That way I became friendly with quite a few people working on commercials. Soon I was taking my portfolio round to the production companies getting myself known. I was asked to work on some of Alan Parker's advertising films, as an assistant in the costume department, and soon I was working on some drama-documentaries.

Probably the most useful thing I did was to join AIP, the Association of Independent Producers. It sounds very high-powered and at first I was very nervous. But they were all terribly helpful and friendly, and after a while — talking to people whom I met through AIP — I realised that there wasn't anything to be frightened about. In fact many of the other members seemed far less street-wise than me. They have been an enormous help. They run seminars, workshops and surgeries where you can talk to two or three experienced people about what you are doing. But probably the most important thing of all that AIP does is that it gives you a chance to meet other people doing the same sort of thing as you — it gives you contacts.

Contacts count 100 per cent. Start off with an idea; even if you do not get that project off the ground, it opens doors and gives you something to talk about to other people. It means that you have something to offer, and it gives you experience in dealing with production companies, money-men, agents, etc. All this means more contacts, and the importance of contacts cannot be overstressed. It means, at times, learning the hard way, but in films the hard way is the best way. It might seem incredibly difficult, but you need to have the mentality of someone doing a jigsaw puzzle: if I can do this then I can do that then I can do the other, etc. If you don't have that kind of mind then don't become a producer.

As far as getting a project off the ground goes, the one golden rule is to work with experienced people, particularly to have a lawyer who understands money. All too often an inexperienced director will work with an inexperienced producer and an inexperienced script-writer . . . and then they wonder why their project never gets off the ground.

The other golden rule is to make a very, very, very good presentation. I'm absolutely horrified at the way I have seen people present things. Recently someone sent me a script and the presentation was absolutely appalling. It wasn't properly typed, the pages were out of order and it was grubby and dirty. It wasn't even in a folder. After a dozen pages I couldn't be bothered to read anymore. It may have been brilliant — though it wasn't — but I just couldn't be bothered.

A good presentation is properly typed and put in a neat folder. It has a neat two-page synopsis, a proper budget breakdown and clear and concise CVs. It is properly packaged and contains no surplus words. After all, the presentation is a test. If you can't get a presentation together then there is no chance that you'll ever be able to get a film together.

Director

The director is responsible for deciding how best to use the technical and artistic resources available. He/she is in charge of directing both the actors and the camera; he/she decides how the film will be mapped out and how best to interpret the script for the camera. The director guides the actors on their interpretation of the part and tells the cameraman what kind of image he/she is looking for. It is vitally important for a director to understand the available resources, such as cameras and lenses, lights and the editing process. A director should have good structural and visual sense. He/she should be able to conceptualise a script and visualise it. Directors need to know what they want to say and how best to say it, using certain images, effects and sounds. The director is in complete charge of the studio or location floor and controls the film artistically, having the final say on all creative matters. The responsibilities of the producer and director sometimes overlap, and often clash. Generally, if the two work well together a production will function smoothly.

CASE STUDY
Sarah, documentary director.

> I fell into film-making through television. After graduating, I got a job at a television station as a researcher. The station gave three of us a chance to direct a film which would be broadcast. After that, they expected us to go on with our old jobs. I knew that I couldn't, and that I wanted to be a free-lance director. So I went off on my own.
>
> I only direct projects I'm interested in, often producing them as well. I can't see the point of being hired in just to tell the cameras what to do. I am not a director who can be hired out to direct other people's ideas. I want to be able to see the content and the visualisation of my projects through shooting and editing.
>
> I prefer doing documentaries because of the human contact involved, and the chance it gives you to relate to other people. Documentaries involve a lot of contact with real people and social issues. For documentary work, you need to be able to talk, listen, and interpret what other people are saying. You give as much as you get. Documentaries are doubly satisfying because you can make a statement — you can educate as well as entertain.

Continuity

The person in charge of continuity is often called the

'script girl', as most of the people responsible for continuity are women. It is a very important job, making certain
that everything, from position of props and clothing to
gestures and voice inflections match from one shot to the
next. The script girl is responsible for the physical continuity of the film. She works closely with the director,
reminding him/her of technical matters, and keeps detailed
notes of each shot. For instance, if an actor's jacket collar
is turned up in one shot, she makes sure it looks the same
in the next. She is there to ensure that the film looks as
if it was shot all at once. A script girl needs a highly
developed sense of observation, and must be able to notice
even the most minor discrepancy. Part of the job is to keep
a detailed log of each day's work, including how long each
shot took, how many retakes were needed and notes on
what problems occurred.

Production Manager

The production manager is responsible for the overall
organisation of the picture under the producer. He/she is, in
effect, the producer's deputy and is actively involved in the
day-to-day problems of filming. It is the production
manager's job to prepare a detailed budget for shooting
during pre-production and a shooting schedule based on
that budget. The production manager works closely with
both the producer and the director.

Once in production, the production manager supervises
the smooth running of the shoot, and is responsible for
such things as contracts being completed correctly, the
hiring of equipment and obtaining permission to film in
certain locations. He/she often acts on behalf of the
producer. It is the production manager's responsibility
to ensure that the film comes in on time and under budget,
using the resources in the most efficient manner possible.

Assistant Director

There are usually three assistant directors: a first, second
and third. Although called assistant directors, they work

more closely with the production department. The first assistant does help the director, but is not the deputy except in crowd scenes.

The first assistant anticipates and carries out the director's practical requirements. He/she supervises the discipline and general organisation of the daily shooting schedule, prepares the call sheets, and liaises with the production manager to make sure the technical needs for the following day's shooting are met. The first assistant is an important link between the production department and the director, often conveying requests from one side to the other. He/she will, however, usually go on to become a production manager rather than a director.

The first assistant will usually hire a second and third to make a team, choosing people he/she feels comfortable working with. The second and third assistants help the first in his/her role. The second assistant usually works more closely with the production office, preparing for the following day's or week's shooting, making sure the cast and equipment needed are ready and available. The third assistant works on the set, and is responsible for ensuring that the artists receive their call and are on the set when needed. He/she helps keep the production running smoothly, and functions very much as the legs of the first assistant.

The assistant directors are responsible for keeping a good working atmosphere on the set, and are responsible to both crew and cast. They are often a barometer of the crew's feelings, letting the director know when the crew are tired or dissatisfied. They are there to maximise the efficiency of the film unit, to foresee and predict problems and to make certain everything comes together for filming with no time being wasted.

CASE STUDY
Bill, assistant director.

> I got my first job through a friend who was a production secretary. She called and asked if I wanted to be a runner on a feature film. A runner is basically an errand boy, getting

cups of tea, delivering scripts, xeroxing — any little thing that has to be done. At that point, during filming, I knew exactly what I wanted to do. It was like a book being opened — a revelation.

Getting the first job was easy. But getting the second job was much harder. When I started working I thought I knew everything, but I now realise how little I actually did know. I didn't take advantage of the people I met and the experience I was gaining.

At the time I started, you had to work as a runner for something like 100 days a year for two or three years before you could apply for a union job. That period is supposed to be your training. You learn about how films are made, what it's like working on a production, what the chain of command is and what each member of the crew does.

Being a runner on a feature film is a great chance to learn. Often you are allowed to do a bit more other than just being a runner, experiencing different areas of production. The chance to learn is unbeatable. I also worked as a runner during pre-production and learned how films are planned and put together.

Working in films is hard — I don't think most people realise this. The hours are long, lots of night shooting during cold, terrible weather. This isn't in any way a nine-to-five job. It takes over your whole life. You get totally absorbed in what you're doing and can't really think about day-to-day living. I can't imagine working in any other career. I love music a lot, and have been lucky enough to work on films that combine the two. That seems to be the best of both worlds.

Lighting Cameraman/Woman

The person doing this job is often called the cinematographer or director of photography. Apart from the director, he/she is the most creative member of the team. He/she works very closely with the director, and is responsible for lighting each shot, choosing camera angles, lenses and filters. The lighting cameraman/woman decides how each shot should look and how best to interpret the director's intentions, but the job does not usually involve positioning or handling the camera.

Camera Operator

The camera operator handles the camera physically for

the lighting cameraman/woman. The two often form a team, going from one production to the next, and their styles are closely united. The operator is responsible for a smooth and efficient camera movement, and attends to the physical details of each shot

There will often be one or two camera assistants. The first, called the focus puller, is in charge of focusing the camera. He/she needs a smooth collaboration with the operator. The focus puller also needs a large degree of technical knowledge.

The second assistant, called the clapper/loader, is in charge of loading and unloading the camera. He/she also fills out the camera sheets with careful records of each shot, including the type of film used, the type of lens and the number of feet of film shot. The clapper/loader also operates the clapper board before each shot.

CASE STUDY

John, lighting cameraman.

I started out as an assistant trainee director for the National Coal Board. Before that, I had gone to medical school for three years and had a number of jobs, including being a bus conductor. I wrote to television stations about training programmes and also to a number of large companies that, at that time, had their own film departments. The Coal Board finally wrote and asked if I was willing to be a trainee assistant director. They did a number of training and safety films about the dangers of machinery and the working conditions in the coal mines. At that time I was more interested in sound and directing, but then it hit me that I wanted to be a cameraman because of the involvement with what you are actually filming.

As other assistants began to leave or be promoted, I finally became a camera assistant. I stayed for about two years, learning as much as I possibly could; then I left the Coal Board and started doing films for local television news and current affairs programmes. During that time I travelled a lot, to Cyprus, Rhodesia and the Middle East. I remember being shot at once, since we covered a lot of political upsets. Travel used to be one of the main attractions of the job, but after you've been to about 50 countries the novelty wears off.

My job changes from production to production. If I'm working on a documentary, there might be just myself and possibly an assistant. The assistant will do lots of things, including operating the camera and adjusting the focus. Sometimes it's just me and the camera and I get to do everything. I actually prefer that. On a commercial, I rarely even get to look through the camera. The director takes an active part and works out the shots with the camera operator. I actually set up the shot and light it, find a good position for the camera and decide on the filters. Though you do get paid more for commercials, I prefer documentaries. You have to be flexible and quick to react. There are a lot of things happening at any one time and it's up to the cameraman to react quickly and spontaneously.

There are more and more women coming into camerawork. I find that women assistants are more conscientious about doing the job properly. They usually know a lot about the equipment and have great ability in handling the camera.

I have a company involving a number of camera and sound personnel. We hire trainees whenever an opening comes up, usually from film school. The students are already aware of the camera and the equipment. You also know that they love film and are serious about working in the industry.

It's sometimes hard to find work, the state of the economy being what it is. Most of mine comes from recommendations or because someone else isn't available. Some cameramen have agents, others have show reels. They take them round to companies and try and sell themselves. You need to have a lot of ambition and drive for that. Most companies tend to use the same crew over and over and you have to be quick to get in there and be in the right place at the right time. A lot of the breaks in this business are due to timing and luck.

Sound Personnel

They rarely work both on location and in a sound studio — the two areas are very different. People working in sound should have an interest in all aspects of sound, including music, and obviously have normal hearing.

SOUND MIXER
He/she is responsible for recording the sound on location and balancing the levels to make sure they are in perspective. The sound mixer usually has an assistant, the sound recordist.

BOOM HANDLER

He/she controls the microphones which are hung out of view of the camera. The position of the mikes is determined by the mixer or recordist.

DUBBING MIXER

This stage of sound is in post-production in a sound studio. The dubbing mixer supervises the recording of additional sound, including music and some sound effects. He/she will also obtain live effects in the studio and record dialogue that was unusable. The dubbing mixer sits on the console and decides the appropriate level of sound, and is responsible for post-synching, that is, matching image to sound. The job is both highly technical and very creative, and it often takes years of experience before becoming a qualified dubbing mixer.

Editor

Though most of an editor's work takes place during post-production, some minor editing may go on during shooting. A director sometimes consults an editor to get the best possible image from a particular shot.

The editor's job is to position the shot, choose the best angles and frames of film and cut them together. He/she is the person who determines the narrative structure of the film, by cutting, editing and assembling the picture. An editor's job is incredibly important – he/she can make or break a picture, having the capacity to correct weak or bad shots or enhance a good one.

The editor usually has two assistants who collect the rushes, put location sound to picture for viewing and also join the cuts together under the supervision of the editor. The assistants keep careful records of each shot. Often the first assistant editor has a great deal of autonomy and responsibility, working almost independently of the supervising editor.

CASE STUDY
Richard, commercials editor.

> In commercials work, editors are usually working for a post-production or editing company. You work on whatever account the company has acquired. In working up to being an editor from a first assistant, you need to bring in clients who are willing to work with you to justify the increase in salary. When I was a first, I did a lot of work on my own, and had a few people who wanted me to cut their films. When I built up a client list, I was made a full editor.

> I started out working for a post-production company as a runner. At that time, I didn't know exactly what I wanted to do. In fact, I thought I might want to be a clapper/loader. All I knew was that I wanted a job that would keep me interested. And my work does.

> I'm never bored with my job. It's very rewarding and very creative. Each stage is different. Because of the number of commercials I might be working on at any one time, and the different stages of editing they might be in, I do a variety of jobs in any one day. On a feature film you work on one film for months before editing is completed.

> Most editors I know work for a specific company, though many well-known editors work freelance, often for the same director over and over again.

> When I first started as a runner, I went all over Soho, learning about the different companies and what they were doing. I made a lot of contacts and learned about film and different techniques involved in editing. The experience for me was invaluable.

Job Discrimination

There are few women and even fewer ethnic minorities represented in the film industry. There have always been traditional 'women's' grades within the union, such as continuity and editing, but until recently there have been few camera technicians or sound personnel. This is changing slowly, mostly due to film schools and also due to the fact that much of the equipment being used is now lighter and easier to handle.

The industry has acknowledged the lack of representation of women and minorities in almost all sectors of film-making with the result that the union is now actively promoting the hiring of women and minorities, and in some cases government funding has been withheld until certain staffing quotas for a production are met. Many of the film schools actively encourage women and minorities to apply, often favouring them over the traditional white male applicants.

Chapter 3

Education and Training

On-the-Job Training

There has been little formalised training in the film industry. Traditionally, training was acquired 'on the job', in a haphazard and fragmented way. You started at the bottom, as a tea boy or messenger, and slowly worked your way up. Some still feel that this type of training is the best, and only, way to learn. Although the experience is valuable, progress is slow, errors can be passed on and the training limited to one field.

Previously, there was more opportunity to move around within the industry and the training received on the job by those now established was far more extensive than the opportunities beginners have today.

Veterans of the industry who learned on the job often have a strong resentment towards film students. They don't want it made too easy for those just starting out. And some people in hiring positions have a bias against film students.

The industry is recognising the need for more training programmes and the union feels strongly that more effective training and education for those entering the film industry will increase their future job prospects.

Case Study
Roger, post-production supervisor.

> I came up through the business by starting as a runner. I worked for over 20 years as a cameraman, and now have my own company.
>
> When I'm looking for someone to hire as a runner, I want somebody young, about 16 or 17, who possibly still lives at

home and doesn't have a lot of expenses. They don't get bored as quickly and are happy just running around. If they show any interest or enthusiasm, they can learn about the company and about editing.

I don't believe film school can give any sort of experience even close to that of working on a real film. You learn this business by working in it. The knowledge you get from film school can be gained by reading books or by making your own short films.

The film schools have little relevance to the industry. The students come out of there thinking they know it all. They want it all quickly and don't want to start at the bottom. I definitely feel on-the-job training is the best. You can't learn at school what you can by working. Sure, you can make little films and have production teams, but it doesn't prepare you for the real problems that arise. You can't substitute education for experience.

Case Study
Matthew, production manager.

I started really young, since I had always known I wanted to work and direct in films. I used to make movies in my spare time on rented equipment.

I wrote to a well-known director, expressing my desire to work with him and learn about the film business. I was lucky and got offered a job as a runner on his new production. At the same time, I found out I had gained a place at film school. But I decided that school wasn't the right route for me and I wanted to be involved in film-making right away. I just couldn't wait. I thought that the experience I would gain by being actively involved in a production would be more useful to me in reaching my goal.

I do feel film schools are helpful, and sometimes wonder if I should have accepted the position. It helps you learn about the various types of films, and gives you an initial, well-rounded training.

If you decide not to go to film school, you really have to love film a lot. You should make small films, study other people's work and teach yourself as much as possible about the business. You have to be determined and really strong, and you have to make sure that you are equal to competing with film school graduates for jobs.

Going to Film School

A big question you might have to decide is, 'Will going to

film school help me get a job?' There is no simple answer. There are still prejudices about film students and the quality of experience gained from film studies. A degree from a film school is no guarantee of a job, no matter how extensive the education.

However, there are a number of reasons for continuing your studies at film school if you are serious about your choice of career. The competition for jobs is getting more and more fierce, and there is an increasing number of film and television studies graduates in the job market. The more knowledgeable and experienced you are, the better are your chances for successfully competing for a job. Film studies will teach you about the different jobs available, give you practical experience in production and will familiarise you with new technology and equipment. It will also give you an understanding of the theory of film and communication and often a historical and critical view as well. Your tutors will be able to introduce you to members of the film industry, who may be helpful when you are looking for work.

It cannot be stressed enough that no school can guarantee employment. There simply are not enough jobs available. However, a degree or diploma from a film school will greatly increase your chances of employment.

Case Study
Mike, editor.

I have my own company, and often when I'm interviewing I realise how helpful film schools are. Graduates have the edge when applying for work.

Depending on the school and the facilities, film studies can really be beneficial. Schools aren't perfect, but then neither is the industry. If students take advantage of the situation, they can learn a lot.

On the practical side, schools give the students a chance to handle film, learn about it and understand how it works. They are usually more interested in working in film than just looking for a job. They tend to be committed and interested.

A lot of people in the industry have feelings of jealousy towards film students. They came up the hard way and expect everyone to. They just don't realise things have changed. The better prepared someone is to do a job, and the more they already know about it, the easier it is on me — I don't have to explain everything.

The industry is notoriously anti-intellectual. Very few people take time to look at other people's work. Film schools give students an opportunity to observe and compare. They get familiar with a number of different styles of film-making. It gives them time to experiment with different ideas. When you're out in the real world, working and hustling for jobs, you don't have the time. In school you have time to think and talk and learn.

Most people without any experience have to start at the bottom, as a runner for example. If you've gone to film school and possibly had a lot of experience in one area, such as camerawork or editing, you can often skip the messenger job and become a trainee or assistant. But you have to be good. And you have to be keen. Just having a degree isn't enough. You have to really love film and have used those three years in school to their best advantage.

The best of the film schools in Britain is undoubtedly the National Film and Television School at Beaconsfield in Buckinghamshire, originally called the National Film School. Nick Broomfield, one of today's outstanding young directors, was one of its first pupils. Here he gives a picture of what it is like to be a student there, and how he was accepted in the first place.

Case Study

Nick, film student.

I made my first film, *Who Cares?*, while I was still at university. I borrowed equipment from a friend who was at Cardiff University. It was an old wind-up Bolex with a zoom lens, so you got only 15 seconds of filming at a time. I had no money so I used to go round to some of the small independent outlets for film. I used to ask for 'short-ends', which was anything from 50 to 100 feet of unused film at the end of the reel. I stuck the ends together and loaded it on a spool, and that's what I shot my first film with. I didn't have to pay anything for film stock. The whole film was like that. I remember the biggest cheque I ever had to write at that time was for the lab bill. It was for £150. Now it seems nothing. My main problem was cutting it. It took a year and a half to cut, though the film was only 18 minutes long.

This was because I had to work in an editing room at night after everyone had gone home. I'd come in at 8.00 pm; my whole life became 'day for night'.

When I applied to film school I realised how important it was to have made a film. It showed — I suppose — that I had initiative and was self-motivated. It let them know what I was interested in and gave the people assessing the applications something to register on. The trouble with most applications is that they are too vague, and the assessors are grappling about, wondering who the applicants are, what they are interested in and how they'd fit in. You've got to remember that in the early days of the School there were only 25 places to be filled each year and there were thousands of applicants. The School spends four months sifting through the applications and the ones they discard at the beginning are the ones where there is nothing to back up the applicants' interests. There is nothing to evaluate them on and unless they have led a very interesting life they don't stand a chance. If you've just come out of school or university then you *must* have something to show them and to show your interest.

If you have got something to back up your application w.th, then there is a good chance that you will get to the interview stage. There you'll find yourself in front of the heads of each of the departments — camera, script, production, direction — together with a student's representative and the head of the school, Colin Young. In the interview the panel will try to find out what each student is interested in. The trouble is that a lot of the applicants don't really know that themselves. They know that they are generally interested in the film industry and that they want to be in it. They have this fantasy — quite inappropriately — that they're going to have a great old time making films. It can't be stressed hard enough what a slog it is. So if you don't know what you are wanting to do, then you don't stand much of a chance, since there are so many people who do.

Originally, all 25 students I was with in the founding year just wanted to make their own films. We were all producers and directors, or at least we wanted to be! Over a period of time natural divisions emerged. One of the criticisms of the early years was that it was all chiefs and no Indians. Everyone wanted to be the next Godard, and since Godard did not hump other people's equipment around, why should they?

There is some theory taught at the National Film School, but the main emphasis is on the practical side. It was highly unstructured as well, though that is changing now. There's a great deal of equipment available so people can go off and make films. Obviously students will make lots of mistakes, but the best way to learn is by the process of error.

One of the most important aspects of the National Film School is that it gets you a union ticket. Getting into the union is one of the most daunting tasks. You can't get a job without being in the union and you can't get in the union without having a job. It's a hopeless situation at first for people who have not got a ticket from film school, and you hear terrible stories of people having to work for two years in a lab in order to get a ticket. After a while, though, you find out ways of getting in. In practice, people say, the union hurdle stops the unimaginative people from getting in, but people with imagination and motivation will always find a way.

What's really useful about film school is that it gives you three years to sort out your ideas, experiment and just find out how everything works. You learn a bit about sound mixing, a bit about editing, and so on. So when you go out into the real world of film no one can turn round and say 'this can't be done.' There is a big mystique built up around films, and a lot of the technicians somewhat resent these 'young whippersnappers' who have come out of film school and who think they know everything. So they make their jobs sound much more complicated than they actually are. But, if you have a practical knowledge, then you can ask reasonable things of them — and you find out that after a while they respect you for it.

There's far less prejudice against film school graduates now than there was ten years ago. Film schools were a completely new phenomenon in the 1970s. Before that you either did a BBC training course or worked your way up through the apprentice system. So there was a feeling that these new film graduates had jumped the queue without paying their dues. And no doubt we were all slightly arrogant. Film schools were teaching new ways of making films, which were more sophisticated and efficient than those used in the industry at the time.

The other problem was that the National Film School, in its early years, was far less structured than it is today. In some ways this was great as it allowed us to be much more creative and to become all-rounders. Now it's much more professional and rigorous. Whether this is better or worse is something we will not know for another ten years, until the people who are now at film school start to make their own films.

Union Recognition of Courses

The ACTT realises that the education and training received at specific schools is equal to an apprenticeship as a messenger or runner. They feel that completion of a three-year full-time course at one of these institutions is equal to intensive practical training.

Three schools have been recognised by the union as providing this training — the National Film and Television School, the London International Film School and the Polytechnic of Central London. Only the Polytechnic has an undergraduate programme. There are other schools under consideration but they will probably not be recognised by the union for some time.

Recognition by the union can be an important factor. As the industry is a closed shop, you cannot work without a union ticket unless there are very special circumstances. Graduates of the recognised schools are basically treated as unemployed members of the union rather than as non-members. Upon graduation, they may apply for any union-graded job. If they are hired, they can apply to the union and the application for membership is granted. They are given a two-year restricted ticket, and receive a full ticket when they get a job in their field.

Applying for Courses

The quality of film studies varies from school to school. Some are geared more towards the practical side of film-making and others are academic, concerned with theory and critique. If you are serious about a career in film, it is important to pick a school that provides a high degree of practical experience. You will benefit more from your schooling and your degree will enhance your employment opportunities. Choose a school that has a good selection of equipment and modern facilities, and one which encourages students to create and experiment. Some schools focus on one or two areas of film-making, such as camera-work or sound. Pick one that best suits your needs.

The competition for places is tough and you should

apply as early as possible. Most schools require a sample of previous work, such as a short film, a script or photographs. They will also require a personal interview, to determine how serious a student is about film studies.

Entry requirements for courses may vary slightly but, generally, applicants must be 18 years or older and possess five GCE passes, two of which should be at A level. Mature students (over 25) without the necessary qualifications are often favourably considered, especially if they have practical experience in film or video. You should contact the school or university concerned for specific information about application dates and entry requirements. (See Part 2 for a list of available courses.)

Chapter 4
Getting Started

Making Contacts

Your first job in the film industry may be the hardest to find. Vacancies for beginners, even those with a film studies degree, are never very numerous. And, depending on the production and economic state of the industry, vacancies may at times be almost non-existent. There are just too many people trying to get into the industry for the number of jobs available.

Only a few positions are advertised in magazines or newspapers. Most people find out about jobs through word of mouth. They hear from a friend or associate that a new production is starting, or they are recommended for a job by someone who has worked with them previously. A lot of it is luck, and being in the right place at the right time. The more people you know, the better your chances of finding employment.

If you have been to university or have had some other form of training, the chances are that your tutors or lecturers will be involved in film and know people working in the industry who may be able to help you. There are also a number of industry organisations that have student membership. They can help put you in touch with other film-makers, give you advice about employment and are useful sources of information in general. They often hold lectures or seminars which give you a good opportunity to meet others in your field. When you meet someone working in film, take their name and number and ask if it would be convenient to call. Most film-makers love their work and are willing to talk to you about their jobs.

Read trade magazines and publications, making a note of new companies being formed or films starting production. Familiarise yourself with names of producers and their companies, and what kinds of movies they make. Do not be afraid to call up companies or write introductory letters, expressing your interest in working for them. They may not have a job, but they will remember your eagerness. You need to show that you are serious about a career in film and are determined to succeed.

Case Study

Linda, continuity.

> To get work, you really have to keep on trying — it's a never-ending battle. With my job, I'm employed from production to production and don't work for one specific company. I'm registered with an agency that sometimes helps me find work. Obviously, if one producer likes your work then your chances of getting another job from him are good. But there are a lot of people out there just like me looking for work, and you're always competing for jobs.
>
> It takes a lot of luck and perseverance. You have to work hard, meeting people and making contacts. You need to keep up to date with what's going on in the industry, what new productions are planned and where new offices are. You need to be there first, letting them know you're available for work.
>
> After a while, a lot of jobs come from people who know you, more so if you're reliable and hard working. But it's tough in the beginning. Read a lot of magazines, like *Screen International*, to find out what's going on. Don't be embarrassed to call up and offer your services. Most of the people you will be talking to started that way and will appreciate your interest. Time is also an important factor. You have to get there first because there are so few jobs. The sooner you can find out about a new production, the better your chances of getting hired. You have to ferret these jobs out before everyone else.
>
> You'll have to be aggressive and determined. Learn not to give up and don't get discouraged. Just keep trying. In this business, if you're out of sight you're out of mind. Be active and keep yourself visible.

Applying for Jobs

'Get in any way you can,' advises Mark Samuelson of the

Association of Independent Producers. 'Get *any* job you can.' When you are first starting, unless you have completed a course at one of the schools recognised by the union, you will need to find a job not restricted to union members. This includes messenger/runner positions and secretarial/clerical jobs. The companies involved in the film industry that you can apply to change from year to year. New ones are constantly being established. There are a number of publications with relatively up-to-date information about the various production and post-production companies. These are listed in Chapter 5.

Production and post-production companies usually have one or two messengers on their staff. They also often hire runners during production. You may need a driving licence for some of these positions. Most companies prefer someone young, about 16 or 17, and living in or around London. They do not pay very well and it is a lot of hard work. But the experience is useful and it is a foot in the door.

The openings are rarely advertised; your best chance is to write to or telephone the various companies, or appear in person, asking about jobs.

Messenger jobs can be a good beginning to your career. Most film companies will give you an opportunity to learn as much as you want, if you show any interest and initiative. From a messenger, you can usually be moved up into a position of more responsibility, such as an assistant or trainee. This may take a long time and do not accept a job thinking that within three to six months you will become an assistant. This occurrence is very rare. The messenger period is intended as an apprenticeship for you to learn more about the industry, more about film-making and how your company operates.

You may also find work as a secretary or receptionist with a production company. This leads to the possibility of moving into production work. Most companies prefer someone aged 18 or older, with good typing and shorthand skills. Some previous office experience would be helpful as a production office can get very hectic and they will want someone organised and responsible. Sometimes these jobs are advertised in local papers and there are employment agencies that deal specifically with the entertainment industry.

Many equipment hire companies employ runners or assistants. Working for one of these companies will provide a good opportunity to learn about the equipment and technology used in film-making, especially if you are interested in camera or sound work. Eventually, a job with one of these companies will lead to your becoming a member of the union, if you are promoted.

The film laboratories used to have extensive training schemes but, with the state of the industry at present, they have been eliminated. Most of the labs are at a constant staffing level, and there are few beginner jobs available. When someone leaves the lab, the position must first be notified to the ACTT. The labs prefer to hire someone already experienced, to avoid the long process involved in training. Only when there is no qualified union member available to fill the position can it be notified externally.

There are occasional trainee positions available, which must first be notified through the ACTT before external advertising. If you have completed a film or television course, your chances of getting a trainee position are much improved. Most companies with a trainee position available prefer to take on someone who is partially trained and already knowledgeable about film. If you are a film school graduate and have specialised in a particular area of film, such as camerawork, editing or sound, you can sometimes get a job as a third assistant or cutting room assistant. But you will have to prove that you have learned something from your schooling and that you are qualified to do the job.

Once you have established yourself at a job, your next step is to apply for membership of the union.

Getting Your Union Ticket

The Association of Cinematograph, Television and allied

Technicians (ACTT) is the main union for most technical/ production jobs in the industry. You cannot apply for most jobs without a union ticket, but you are not eligible for union membership until you have found a job. It sounds like a vicious circle, but it is not as complicated as it appears. The union is there to protect the interests of its members by being restrictive. With the high unemployment in the industry, they are concerned and try to deter all but the most keen and determined newcomer.

When you have found a company willing to hire you, or if you are already employed and the company is willing to promote you to a union-graded job, the company will sponsor you for union membership. If accepted, you will be granted a two-year restricted ticket. During that two-year period, you must continue working for your sponsor company. After that period, the restriction is lifted and you are given a full ticket. You may then change places of employment or change jobs, such as becoming a third assistant director from an assistant editor.

If you have graduated from one of the union-recognised film schools, you can apply for union membership when you have found a job. You will receive the two-year restricted ticket, and are then eligible for a full ticket when you find a job in your chosen field.

Most companies employing over a certain number of employees have their own chapters, or 'shops', within the union and hold regular meetings. The union also has shops for the freelance sector, being divided by job, such as director, editor, cameraman, etc. It is a good idea to attend these meetings to find out what is going on within the industry and the relations between your area of film and the union.

Union representatives are more than willing to talk to you about your career and will offer advice and information and, it is to be hoped, some encouragement.

Freelance Work

Until recently, most positions within the union were

considered freelance, or self-employed. Some jobs may last the length of the production, which in the case of commercials might be only a day or two. You will probably work in more than one area of film-making within a single year, and for a number of different companies.

But the tax laws changed in 1983 and now most of these positions are considered full-time employment. You should find yourself a qualified accountant as soon as you are employed to help you with your tax. One of your associates should be able to recommend an accountant familiar with film and entertainment tax laws.

If you are considered by the Inland Revenue to be self-employed, you are responsible for paying your own tax and National Insurance stamps as well as being ineligible for sick pay. In other cases your employer will take care of this for you.

The union has detailed information relating to the tax status of its members, and your accountant will be able to sort out this complicated problem for you.

Part 2

Chapter 5
Courses Available

Guide to Courses

The courses are divided into three sections. Section One deals with schools and universities in which practical work in film and video constitutes a major part of the courses. Detailed information is given on the structure of each course.

Section Two lists schools which have film and television training, though some of the courses are theoretical rather than practical. They tend to stress the creative use of the media and do not provide vocational training as such. You should consult the school for detailed information about the course. Section Three lists postgraduate courses and provides detailed information.

The subject of film studies is becoming more extensive and the courses are improving yearly. Many schools are instituting more extensive facilities and equipment. For the most up-to-date information, contact the school for specific details about courses and application requirements.

Section One

Bournemouth and Poole College of Art and Design
School of Photography/Film Production, Royal London House, Lansdowne, Bournemouth BH1 3JL; 0202 207772
Higher Diploma in Photographic Media Studies
The course covers all aspects of professional film and television studies. First-year students receive an introduction to photography, film and audio-visual studies. In their third term students choose their option of study. Film option

students undertake a larger proportion of film-biased studies. Second-year students work on a film from shooting through to post-production. Third-year students conceive and direct a film by themselves.

In 1983, Bournemouth and Poole College joined the 'Adopt-a-Student' scheme, pioneered by Harrow College of Further Education, to give students a year's leave. The students spend this year with a production company, gaining practical experience.

Derbyshire College of Higher Education
School of Art and Design, Kedleston Road, Derby DE3 1GB; 0332 47181
BA (Hons) Photographic Studies
Over half the course work is practical rather than theoretical. Students work creatively in all aspects of film and photography. In Part 2 of the course students assume considerable responsibility for individual work programmes. The course seeks to recruit a wide range of students and some emphasis is placed on mature students, who may make up for a lack of formal entry requirements in terms of experience and a proven commitment to the photographic arts.

Harrow College of Higher Education
Faculty of Art and Photography, Northwick Park, Harrow, Middlesex HA1 3TP; 02-864 5422
BA (Hons) Applied Photography, Film and Television
The primary aim of the course is to establish students' ability to apply film and photography to the processes of communication. The first year is common study with both film and photography students. In the second year film students specialise in either commercial and cultural applications of film and television, or scientific and industrial applications of film and television. The first option is especially concerned with using film in commercial, sociological and community contexts. Students are encouraged to develop their technical competence and abilities and are encouraged to pursue individual talents such as scriptwriting, directing, camerawork and sound. They learn to function as a member of a cooperative team. The course is

geared towards professional training, and almost 75 per cent of the studies is practical work. The scientific and industrial applications course is concerned with the uses of film for objective illustration, visualisation and document-ation. It deals mainly with the use of film in solving problems in science, medicine, industry and education.

In 1983, Harrow College started a new scheme in association with Harlech TV called 'Adopt-a-Student' by which individual television and film companies take on students for one year during their course to gain practical experience. The scheme has now been taken up by the University of Bristol, Newport Film School and Bournemouth and Poole College of Art and Design.

London College of Printing
Department of Photography, Film and Television, Elephant and Castle, London SE1 6SB; 01-735 8484
BA (Hons) Photography, Film and Television
The course is intended to develop visual awareness and creative thinking. The first year is non-specialised study, and is intended to familiarise students with the common languages of all three media, as well as the mechanics of production and the technical processes and materials used. Students choose a course of study in the second year, with opportunities to gain practical experience in their area of study. The third year is spent in achieving an integration of ideas and technique with visual style. Students are expected to develop an individual body of work that is both coherent and professional. A major part of the study is practical and the school is fully equipped with up-to-date facilities.

Manchester Polytechnic
Faculty of Art and Design, Capitol Building, School Lane, Didsbury, Manchester M20 0HT; 061-434 3331
BA (Hons) Design for Communication Media/Film and Television Studies
This course provides a full-time specialisation in film and television production. Over 80 per cent of the course is practical work and based on project-centred activity. The aim is to give students a practical knowledge of the

fundamental methods of creating programmes in sound and vision. During the first year students gain experience in both design and production, including directing a short television sequence and learning camera techniques. During the second and third years students may bias their work towards opportunities in the industry, education or broadcasting. In the third year students carry out at least one major production.

Polytechnic of Central London
School of Communication, 18-22 Riding House Street, London W1P 7PD; 01-486 5811
BA (Hons) Film and Photography
The school places as much emphasis on theory as on practical work and the course is divided evenly between the two. In the first year students follow a general introductory course in both film and photography. In the second year students specialise, with film students working in small production groups on two practical projects designed to help them express their ideas in film. In the third year the practical work is on major film projects, devised, scripted, budgeted and produced by the students themselves. A large number of graduates go on to obtain employment in the film industry.

Sheffield City Polytechnic
Faculty of Art and Design, Brincliffe, Psalter Lane, Sheffield S11 8UZ; 0742 56101
BA (Hons) Fine Art, Communication Arts
The Communication Arts programme covers new media that have made an impact on fine art over the last 15 years. This includes film, photography, video and performance art. After an initial year spent comparing how each medium operates, students specialise in the second and third years. No pressure is put on students to limit their work to any one medium. Film productions range from short 8mm films to 16mm documentaries and small 35mm productions. There are excellent professional facilities for shooting, processing, editing and dubbing. The school also has well-equipped video and sound studios.

West Surrey College of Art and Design
Department of Audio-Visual Studies, Falkner Road, The
Hart, Farnham, Surrey GU9 7DS; 0252 722441
BA (Hons) Photography, Film and Video, Animation
The course is essentially practical, designed to encourage a
direct and fundamental appraisal of photography, film,
video and animation.

Part 1 of the course aims to develop an understanding of
the basic concept of each medium. Workshops introduce
practical skills, and a programme of theoretical study
considers historical and critical issues. Students work
within their chief area of study in Part 2. They develop
the appropriate techniques and practical skills needed.
Part 3 is devoted to in-depth study within individual work
programmes. Film and video students will spend a significant
part of their study in production teams.

Section Two

University of Birmingham
Faculty of Humanities, PO Box 363, Birmingham
B15 2TT; 021-472 1301

Bretton Hall College
Media Department, West Bretton, Wakefield, West Yorkshire
WF4 4LG; 0924 85261

College of Ripon and York St John
Lord Mayor's Walk, York YO3 7EX; 0904 56771

Croydon College
School of Art and Design, Fairfield, Croydon CR9 1DX;
01-688 9271

University of East Anglia
School of English and American Studies, Norwich
NR4 7TJ; 0603 56161

University of Exeter
American & Commonwealth Arts Section, School of
English, Queen's Building, The Queen's Drive, Exeter
EX4 4QH; 0392 77911

University of Glasgow
Department of Drama, 17 Lilybank Gardens, Glasgow
G12 8RZ; 041-339 8855

Goldsmiths' College
Department of Visual Communication, Lewisham Way,
New Cross, London SE14 6NW; 01-692 7171

Gwent College of Higher Education
Faculty of Art and Design, Clarence Place, Newport,
Gwent NPT 0UW; 0633 59984

Hatfield Polytechnic
School of Humanities, PO Box 109, College Lane, Hatfield,
Hertfordshire AL10 9AB; 07072 68100

Hull College of Higher Education
School of Design, Queen's Gardens, Hull HU1 3DH;
0482 224121

University of Hull
Department of Drama, Cottingham Road, Hull HU6 7RX;
0482 46311

University of Kent
Rutherford College, Canterbury, Kent C12 7NX;
0227 66822

Lanchester Polytechnic
Faculty of Art and Design, Gosford Street, Coventry
CV1 5RZ; 0203 24166

Leeds Polytechnic
School of Creative Arts and Design, Calverley Street,
Leeds LS1 3HE; 0532 462439

Liverpool Polytechnic
Faculty of Art and Design, Hope Street, Liverpool
L1 9EB; 051-709 9711

University of Liverpool
Centre for Communication Studies, Chatham Street,
Liverpool L69 3BX; 051-709 6022

University of Manchester
Department of Drama, Oxford Road, Manchester M13 9PL;
061-273 3333

Middlesex Polytechnic
Centre for Film and Television, Cat Hill, Barnet,
Hertfordshire EN4 8HU; 01-440 7431

Newcastle upon Tyne Polytechnic
Faculty of Art and Design, Squires Building, Sandyford
Road, Newcastle upon Tyne NE1 8ST; 0632 326002

University of Newcastle upon Tyne
Department of English Language and Literature, Newcastle
upon Tyne NE1 7RU; 0632 328511

North Staffordshire Polytechnic
Department of Art History and Complementary Studies,
College Road, Stoke-on-Trent ST4 2DE; 0782 45531

Portsmouth Polytechnic
Department of Historical and Literary Studies, Kings
Rooms, Bellevue Terrace, Southsea PO5 3AT; 0705 827681

University of Stirling
Stirling FK9 4LA; 0786 3171

University of Strathclyde
Film and Television Studies, Livingstone Tower, Glasgow
G1 1XH; 041-552 4400

Sunderland Polytechnic
Department of Languages and Culture, Forster Building,
Chester Road, Sunderland SR2 7EE; 0783 76191

Ulster Polytechnic
School of Art and Design, Research, History and Criticism,
York Street, Belfast BT15 1ED; 0232 228515

New University of Ulster
Coleraine, Co Londonderry BT52 1SA; 0265 4141

University of Warwick
Joint School of Film and Literature, Coventry CV4 7AL;
0203 24011

Section Three

University of Bristol

Department of Drama, 29 Park Row, Bristol BS1 5LT;
0272 24161

Postgraduate Certificate in Radio, Film and Television

This is a one-year intensive course in radio, film and television production. Each year the course produces a half-hour programme for the BBC as well as having a show of work at the National Film Theatre. Admission to the course is by interview and submission of work. Some prior knowledge of media or media aptitude is assumed.

Croydon College

School of Art and Design, Barclay Road, Croydon CR9 1AX; 01-688 9271

Diploma Certificate in Intermedia Studies

A one-year intensive course in film, television and animation. Applicants must normally be diplomates or graduates in related studies, or have professional experience in film, television or animation. The course is aimed at students in associated fields as well as those with practical experience in film or television.

Goldsmiths' College

Department of Visual Communication, Lewisham Way, New Cross, London SE14 6NW; 01-692 7171

Diploma in Art and Design (Communication Studies)

This one-year full-time course has a practical, theoretical and research focus on all the recognised media of communication. Students are able to spend 50 per cent of their time on practical work, and there is a possibility of specialising in television broadcasting.

London International Film School

24 Shelton Street, London WC2H 9HP; 01-240 0168

The London International Film School is privately run and funded entirely on students' fees. It specialises in technical work, turning out editors, sound recordists and animators. The students learn every aspect of film-making, and gain a well-rounded understanding of all the processes involved. The school emphasises a hands-on policy, familiarising students with equipment. The average number of students accepted per year is 25. The programme is two years long and although most of the students have a first degree, this requirement is not strictly adhered to. If an applicant shows a creative track record, either in school or professionally, certain entry requirements can be waived.

Middlesex Polytechnic
Faculty of Art and Design, Cat Hill, Barnet, Hertfordshire EN4 8HU; 01-440 7431
Postgraduate Diploma in Film and Television Studies
This one-year course accepts 15 students per year and early application is advised. It is designed to offer an integrated programme of study in both film and television, and theory and practice have equal value in the course.

National Film and Television School
Beaconsfield Film Studios, Station Road, Beaconsfield, Buckinghamshire; 04946 71234
The National Film and Television School was established in 1970. It is a non-profit-making institution and is funded by the government. It is probably the best equipped school, and the most highly regarded professionally.

The three-year programme concentrates on the practical side of film-making. The school functions as a postgraduate course, although first degrees are not a requirement of admission. The average age of the students is slightly higher than usual. They have a strong professional and practical outlook on their studies and may have already been employed in the film industry in some capacity. The students are very serious about film and their careers — the courses are not in any way intended for beginners.

Applicants are required to submit samples of their work or to demonstrate proven ability in one or more areas of the primary instruction of the school, including writing, directing, producing or photography. Only 25 applicants are accepted per year, with five of these places being held for overseas applicants.

Royal College of Art
School of Film and Television, Queens Gate, London SW7 2EU; 01-584 5020
MA (RCA) Film and Television Production Courses
This full-time three-year course accepts 15 students per year. Students must already have the necessary background in film, animation or television production. Workshops are conducted in preparation of short films, animation and television and video work. All applicants must submit not more than 30 minutes of film or video work. A major part of the course is practical, with students specialising in the area of their choice. They are introduced to the techniques of cameras, lights, sound and editing. In the first year the technical standards of the students are reinforced and in the second and third years students are expected to prepare and produce films and videos.

Film Workshops

There are a number of independent organisations, including art centres, film co-operatives and collectives which have film and video equipment and facilities available for public use. Many can offer information and advice, as well as holding evening classes in film and video production.

The 1980s have seen a great expansion in workshop productions, thanks partially to Channel 4 which has almost doubled the sums previously available to film workshops, and to the ACTT's 'Workshop Declaration' which gives accreditation to production-based non-profit-making workshops employing more than four people. The British Film Institute's Production Board provides finance for specific projects.

Following is a list of film co-operatives and workshops, but you should contact the workshops directly for details of their facilities and training opportunities.

For more information on setting up workshops and receiving funds, contact: Barnie Ellis Jones, Head of Projects, BFI (Distrib), 127 Charing Cross Road, London WC2H 0EA; 01-437 4355.

England

Amber Films
5 Side, Newcastle upon Tyne; 0632 322000

Bath Arts Workshop
Widcombe Institute, Widcombe Hill, Bath BA2 6AA;
    0225 310154

Workshop Film, c/o Oliver Tringham, 20 Henrietta Street,
    Bath

146 Walcott Street, Bath, Avon; 0225 310154

Berwick Street Film Collective
7-9 Earlham Street, Covent Garden, London WC2;
01-240 2350

Birmingham Film Workshop
Triangle Arts, Holt Street, Birmingham B7 4BA;
021-359 4192

Bradford Communications Centre
21 Chapel Street, Bradford; 0274 341486

Bradford Film Group
c/o Bradford Film Theatre, Chapel Street, Bradford;
0274 720329

Bristol Film Co-op
37-9 Jamaica Street, Bristol BS2 8JP; 0272 426199

Cinema Action
27 Winchester Road, Swiss Cottage, London NW3;
01-586 2762

Colchester Film Workshop
The Minories, 74 High Street, Colchester, Essex CO1 1UE;
0206 77067

East Anglian Film-Makers Co-op
Cinema City, St Andrew's Street, Norwich NR2 4AD;
0603 22313

Exeter Film Workshop
Kintor, Poughill, Crediton, Devon; 03636 420

Film Forum
65 Dunstanburgh Close, Washington, Tyne and Wear;
0632 467733

Film Work Group
79-89 Lots Road, London SW10; 01-352 0538

Four Corner Films
113 Roman Road, Bethnal Green, London E2 0HU;
01-981 4243

Hull Film Co-op
Postern Gate Gallery, 6 Postern Gate, Hull; 0482 24813

Huntingdon Film Workshop
Huntingdon College, California Road, Huntingdon,
Cambridgeshire PE18 7BL; 0480 52346

Ipswich Film Workshop
Suffolk College, Department of Art and Design, High Street,
Ipswich, Suffolk IP1 3QH; 0473 55885

Leeds Animation Workshop
45 Bayswater Row, Leeds; 0532 484997

Leeds Film Group
191 Bellevue Road, Leeds; 0532 490856

Liberation Films
2 Chichele Road, London NW2; 01-450 7855

London Film-makers' Co-op
42 Gloucester Avenue, London NW1; 01-586 4806

Luton Film Workshop
Luton Community Arts Trust, 33 Guildford Street, Luton,
Bedfordshire; 0582 419584

Manchester Film and Video Workshop
5 James Leigh Street, Manchester M60 1SX; 061-236 6953

New Cinema Workshop
Midland Group Nottingham, 24-32 Carlton Street,
Nottingham NG1 1NN; 0602 582636/583489

Newsreel Collective
c/o The Other Cinema, 79 Wardour Street, London W1;
01-734 8508

North East Films
Hollinhush, Dale Head, Rosedale, Near Pickering, North
Yorkshire; 07515 269

Open Eye Film and Video
90-2 Whitechapel, Liverpool; 051-709 9460

Oxford Film Workshop
The Stables, Bury Knowle East, North Place, Headington,
Oxford; 0865 60079

Portsmouth Film and Video Workshop
John Pound Centre, St James Street, Portsmouth;
0705 743366

Sheffield Independent Film Group
173 Howard Road, Walkley, Sheffield; 0742 336429

Sheffield Women's Film Co-op
Albreda House, Lybgate Lane, Sheffield S10 5SH;
0742 668857

Southill Park Film Workshop
Southill Park, Bracknell, Berkshire; 0344 27272

St Edmund's Film Workshop
St Edmund's Art Centre, Bedwin Street, Salisbury,
Wiltshire; 0722 20379

Stoke Film Workshop
64 Nelson Street, Fenton, Stoke-on-Trent ST4 3QP

Thamesdown Film Workshop
The Arts Centre, Devizes Road, Swindon, Wiltshire;
0793 26161 ext 3133

Trade Films
7 Woodbine Terrace, Gateshead NE8 1RU; 0632 770085

Women in Moving Pictures
50 St Andrew's Road, Montpelier, Bristol

Workers Film Association
9 Lucy Street, Manchester; 061-848 9782

York Film
8 The Crescent, Blossom Street, York; 0904 27129

Wales

Chapter Film Workshop
Market Road, Canton, Cardiff; 0222 396061

Community Video Workshop
36 Tudor Street, Riverside, Cardiff; 0222 396061

Gweld Video
Uned 4, Gweithdai Maenofferen, Blaenau Ffestiniog,
Gwynedd; 0766 89382

Wrexham Community Video Project
Church House, Rhosddu Road, Wrexham, Clwyd;
0978 264051

Additional Training Opportunities

In 1981, Hilary Coutt was commissioned by the National
Film and Television School to report on the need for
additional training in the film industry. The results of her
research show that, among ACTT members, 50 per cent
entered the industry without any training but 70 per cent
felt that training on entry was necessary; 87 per cent
received no additional training but 82 per cent felt that
they wanted further training. Among employers, 92 per
cent felt that there should be an industry-wide training
scheme.

A few intensive training courses exist, but the best ones
are over-subscribed, and most are limited to people who
have already had some experience in the film industry.
By far the best of the intensive courses in film-making
and video today is run by Crosswind Films Ltd (3 Soho
Square, London W1V 5DE; 01-439 1973/4/5). Set up in
1978 to give clandestine instruction to BBC cameramen
in new techniques, it has expanded into what is essentially
a 'film crammers'. It is run by a collective of freelance
film directors, cameramen, sound recordists and lighting

specialists, and gives a series of intensive courses ranging from one day, through one week, to three weeks, with longer part-time and weekend courses running over ten weekends. Almost all the training is practical, and Crosswind has some of the best equipment for film students in the country.

Steve Bernstein, the principal, believes in total immersion, with 12- to 16-hour days, both in general filmmaking and in specialised subjects such as direction, camera work, sound recording, lighting and editing. For many who have been through the courses, it has become a qualification for entry both to the National Film and Television School and to jobs in the industry.

The numbers taken on are small (only ten pupils per course) with an extremely high proportion of teachers to students. Competition for enrolment is high, with five applications for every place.

'When we look at the applications,' says Bernstein, 'we are not interested in the rich kids who just want to play. Intelligence and motivation are what we are looking for, and particularly people who have been on the fringes of the industry and have shown by their past efforts that they are really enthusiastic. We're not really interested in school-leavers who have done nothing — unless they are very special. To school-leavers who haven't done anything, my advice would be to try and get a job somewhere — anywhere — in the film industry, even making tea, and then come back to us after a couple of years.'

Inevitably, with such good equipment and such a high proportion of tutors to pupils, fees are high. Week-long immersion courses and part-time, ten-weekend courses cost £560. Three-week intensive courses cost £1000, weekend courses cost £175 and day courses cost £75. Indeed, at these prices selection itself becomes easy — anyone who can save up that amount of money to learn about films *must* be motivated.

Another excellent series of intensive courses is now being run by the National Film and Television School at Beaconsfield. So far the school has run ten courses, on video familiarisation (one course reserved exclusively for ethnic minorities and another reserved exclusively for women) and acting in front of the camera.

The Association of Independent Producers' administrator, Fiona Halton, went on the production management course and reported on it in AIP's magazine, *AIP and Co*: 'What impressed me was the sense of industry talking to industry; years of experience came tumbling out in each of the lectures. My over-riding feeling was that there were not enough hours in the day to cram everything in. Students on other courses apparently felt the same . . . We covered everything from scheduling and budgeting (with production managers and accountants as speakers) to the trade union agreements (with representatives from all the relevant unions). A vital ingredient in the success of the course is the methodical way in which all the major topics in the syllabus are treated.'

The Association of Professional Recording Studios runs an excellent one-week course in sound recording. It provides information on a wide variety of subjects relating to sound and sound recording, and includes demonstrations of modern equipment. The course, held in September at the University of Surrey, is of a fairly high level. Though no academic qualifications are needed to register, a certain amount of basic technical knowledge is assumed. For more information about the course, contact the APRS at 23 Chestnut Avenue, Chorleywood, Hertfordshire WD3 4HA.

Kodak Limited runs a series of motion picture and television courses at their Marketing Education Centre in Hemel Hempstead. The courses, generally one to three days, are of a very high standard. The centre has excellent facilities, including work and dark rooms, laboratories and projection facilities. Trainees come from all over Britain and are usually sponsored by production companies, other labs and television stations. The courses are open to students, though some prior knowledge of film is assumed. Some of the courses are highly technical, dealing with the properties of film itself and quality control, and others are excellent training for anyone wanting to learn more about film and its uses. For detailed information about the courses, contact Kodak Limited, Motion Picture Sales, PO Box 66, Hemel Hempstead, Hertfordshire HP1 1JU; 0442 62331.

There are a number of other private schools and courses which offer classes in film and video, although the standards vary with the schools. Although some of these schools do offer excellent training, you should investigate their facilities and tuition before committing yourself and enrolling.

Both the BBC and ITV companies have film training programmes. Film plays a major role in many television programmes, and some broadcasts consist entirely of filmed material. To start at the BBC you would enter as a trainee. These positions are advertised in *The Listener* as well as specialist publications and local newspapers. You must be at least 18 years old, with O levels or the equivalent, and have a keen interest in film or sound recording. Normal colour vision is essential and normal hearing is necessary for sound assistants. A current driving licence may also be required. You will be trained as an assistant in film camerawork, sound recording or editing. The training programme, which lasts about a year, includes both formal instruction and practical experience. Trainees are promoted to assistant status after training and on passing a proficiency test and subject to satisfactory training reports. Promotion for more senior jobs is by competition for internally advertised vacancies.

The ITV companies also hire a small number of trainees per year, usually in editing, camera and sound. The positions are advertised in magazines such as *Studio Sound*, as well as local newspapers, and film schools are notified of the openings. They are looking for applicants aged around 22 years or older, with a background in film, which is why they tend to prefer film school students or graduates. The training programme lasts about nine months, with an assessment every three months. If accepted, trainees are absorbed into the company and receive a full ticket from the ACTT.

Chapter 6

Opportunities Abroad

'There has probably never been more incentive than there is at this moment for Britain's bright young film-makers to go west,' wrote producer Simon Perry in *Sight And Sound* (summer 1980), 'joining what the National Film Finance Corporation's managing director, Mamoun Hassan, calls "not so much a brain drain but a soul drain".'

Job opportunities may be limited in Britain, but beware of thinking that the grass is greener on the other side. It is equally parched. Often it is harder to get jobs abroad, since you are not operating in your own environment, and the whole process of building up contacts — essential in the film industry — is that much more difficult. The only real justification in looking for work abroad is that you want to live abroad. Then the best thing you can do is go abroad and start from there. To some people, particularly the adventurous, the challenge of living and working abroad is attractive. For them, here is a brief guide to opportunities in the English-speaking world.

United States

The USA is the capital of the world's film industry, employing over 200,000 people, compared with the 10,000 employed in Britain. There are also more film schools in the USA than anywhere else in the world, with over 35,000 film and television graduates entering the market every year. *The American Film Institute Guide to College Courses in Film and Television* (Book Order Department, Peterson's Guides, Department 7591, PO Box 978, Edison, NJ 08817

USA) gives listings of all US and Canadian film schools, but write to the individual colleges for details of what they specialise in before committing yourself; they do not only provide a variety of theoretical and practical training, but will give you your first 'wave' of contacts, essential for starting off on your career. So make sure that the school you apply to gives you not only the training you want, but also the right geographical location for what you want to specialise in. If you want to go into feature films, for example, then go to a school in southern California, so you'll be in the right place to start off on your career. The following selection of some of the best schools gives some idea of the variety of courses being offered.

School of Public Communication, Boston University offers courses in broadcasting and film, with training in screenwriting, direction, animation, TV production and multi-media presentation. (Contact Peter Ladue, Director of Film Production Program, Boston University, School of Public Communication, 640 Commonwealth Avenue, Boston, Massachusetts 02215, USA.)

New York University offers graduate and undergraduate courses in film-making and also has a summer school in which veteran film-makers teach general film-making, sound, editing, lighting and screenwriting courses. (Contact the Office of Admissions, New York University, 25 West 4th Street, Washington Square, New York, NY 10003, USA.)

Monroe Community College in Rochester, New York State, offers a two-year specialist course in film and video equipment. It is almost entirely practical and technically orientated.

Columbia College Chicago specialises in production courses for film, television, radio and advertising, as well as courses in animation, scriptwriting, editing and sound. These are all of a practical rather than theoretical nature.

The University of Texas, Austin, has an introductory course in image and sound, and advanced courses in directing, cinematography, sound editing, film editing and video. Its most interesting course is the technical one in electronics in the media, which covers system designs, instrumentation and 'troubleshooting'. Considering that the technical and electronic aspects of film-making are the least over-subscribed, and offer some of the best job opportunities, it is probably one of the most worthwhile courses for British students to consider.

The University of California, Los Angeles, has the largest film school in the world, with courses in production, acting, cinematography, sound recording, editing, writing, animation and directing, as well as a summer school in television studies.

The University of Southern California concentrates on practical studies, with all students making their own films. The fact that for each of the last 20 years at least one graduate's film has been nominated for an Academy Award gives some idea of the high standards of the college. There are courses in production design, script analysis, laboratory work, animation and special effects. The University of Southern California also has a six-week summer school with students spending 40 per cent of their time at Universal Studios, Hollywood.

One of the most attractive aspects of film schools in the States is the large number of summer schools and workshops that are available, which many foreign students are able to combine with a US vacation. The American Film Institute runs a series of workshops in the summer vacation at Boston, Chicago, Dallas, Los Angeles, New York, San Francisco and Washington. Kodak also runs workshops at Atlanta, Chicago, Dallas, Hollywood, New York, Rochester and San Francisco. For more information on workshops see *The American Film Institute Guide to College Courses in Film and Television*.

One way to find work in the US, once you have gone to live there and established contacts, is through the cable and satellite community TV stations which are now mushrooming. But the main hurdle to working in the States, as in Britain, is the unions. It is impossible, however, to detail specific ways of gaining entry. Union agreements vary state by state and film studio by film studio, and there is no one union that dominates all others, like the ACTT in Britain.

Canada

The Canadian film industry is dominated by the National Film Board of Canada, set up by John Grierson in 1939 'to initiate and promote the production and distribution of films in the national interest . . . and in particular . . . to interpret Canada to Canadians and other countries', which employs over 1000 people. Originally, the films sponsored by the National Film Board of Canada were documentaries, which was inevitable given Grierson's guiding spirit. In recent years, though, the NFB has sponsored an increasing number of features, among them Claude Jutra's *Mon Oncle Antoine* in 1972, which some consider to be Canada's finest film.

In spite of the work of the NFB, the US still dominates the Canadian film industry. It was to offset this that the Canadian Government legislated for a 100 per cent capital cost allowance to encourage Canadians to invest in Canadian films. But any jobs that materialise from this legislation will mostly be taken up by Canadians themselves. Virtually all NFB employees and film-makers sponsored by the NFB are Canadian. In short, jobs in the Canadian film industry are hard to find, but for those who are determined enough to look for them, they are there, though hidden, particularly in the growing cable and pay-TV industry. Those interested in Canadian film schools should consult *The American Film Institute Guide to College Courses in Film and Television*.

Australia

The 1970s saw a flowering of the Australian film industry. Between 1970 and 1980, 120 Australian feature films were made with some, like *Picnic at Hanging Rock* (1977) and *My Brilliant Career* (1979), being financial as well as critical successes. In 1982, a total of 22 feature films were made, which was comparable to the number made in the UK with its much larger industry.

As far as jobs go, feature film-making is the hardest to break into. There are far more opportunities in the hundreds of small films and documentaries made by production companies, of which there are more than 300 in Australia. One of the conventional ways into the film industry is now closed in Australia; since 1960, all Australian commercials have to be shot by Australian crews.

Australia does have the first-rate Australian Film and Television School near Sydney, established in 1973, with three-year courses in directing, production, camerawork, sound recording and editing. Applicants do not have to be Australian nationals, but they must be residents at the time of application. Last year there were over 12 applications for every place. The school also has open programmes for those who have already had practical experience in film and television. For more details write to: The Recruitment Office, Australian Film and Television School, Box 126 PO, North Ryde, New South Wales 2113, Australia.

Chapter 7

Organisations, Unions, Production Companies and Publications

There are a number of industry organisations made up of members who are actively involved in film-making. Some are open to students, and others are open only to those professionally experienced in a particular field.

The organisations are great sources of information, especially for beginners. They often have newsletters and handbooks, run lectures and seminars and generally keep their members informed on the industry as a whole.

Following is a list of organisations, unions and production companies that will be helpful in reaching your goal. They are all more than willing to talk to beginners, and will usually put you in touch with one of their members who can offer advice and assistance. Contact the organisations direct for complete information about membership requirements, application fees and services provided.

Organisations

Association of Independent Producers (AIP)
17 Great Pulteney Street, London W1R 3DG; 01-743 1581
The Association of Independent Producers was established in 1976, 'a shoe-string organisation dedicated to helping people to make silk purses out of shoe-strings', as AIP vice-chairman James Brabazon calls it. There are now over 450 members, all of whom are active in the film business. In spite of its title, AIP is not limited to producers. Its facilities are open to anyone who works in film and needs its services. It has widespread membership throughout

the industry, taking its members from almost every sector.

AIP provides an information service which is available only to members. It works as a clearing house, enabling producers, directors and writers to get in touch with each other. It publishes an excellent monthly newsletter, *AIP and Co*, which contains film producer Alan Parker's hilarious cartoons about the British cinema (the cartoons alone are worth the subscription and should be published as a book in their own right), and first-rate features and articles on the film industry, as well as a yearly producer's handbook. AIP also sponsors a number of seminars on film production and finance. Membership costs £75 per year and is well worth it (though students and 'unwaged' producers — whatever that means — can join for £40). The organisation's most useful role is helping beginners to make contacts, and encouraging them to build up confidence in themselves and their abilities. With that goes its role in giving advice and information. In addition it acts as a lobby to increase government support for the film industry and to protect independent producers from both the US and from the major production companies in Britain.

It is a friendly and approachable organisation and as well as running seminars it holds regular 'surgeries' for its members. These give young and inexperienced film-makers the opportunity to talk over their ideas with experienced producers and directors in complete confidence. 'We found it very helpful and useful,' AIP members Alistair Wayne and Alan Phillips have said of the surgeries, 'though the 20 minutes went by like two seconds. It's a lovely service to provide for those who are moving into the industry . . . a superb leg-up.' (*AIP and Co*, September 1983)

British Academy of Film and Television Arts (BAFTA)
195 Piccadilly, London W1; 01-734 0022
BAFTA was formed in 1946 by British film-makers as a non-profit-making company. It aims to advance the art and technique of film and encourages research and experimentation. Membership is restricted to those who have made a creative contribution to the industry or plan to commence a production within 12 months of joining. BAFTA has

screening facilities, holds regular seminars, lectures and discussion meetings and it holds an annual awards ceremony which is broadcast on television.

British Film Fund Agency (BFFA)
9 Cavendish Square, London W1M 9DD; 01-353 2741
Financed by the Eady Levy, whereby every cinema exhibitor must contribute one-twelfth of all box office receipts to the Fund, the money finances the National Film and Television School, the British Film Institute Production Board and film productions. Unfortunately, the amount given to each production depends on its box office success; thus the rich get richer and the poor get nowhere. The system has been much criticised, particularly since it pays no heed to quality, and allows foreign companies to milch Eady through pseudo-British subsidiaries. How long the BFFA is likely to survive is a very open question.

British Film Institute
127 Charing Cross Road, London WC2H 0EA; 01-437 4355
The British Film Institute was established in 1933 to encourage the development of the art of film and television. The BFI provides a number of services. Their library is an information and study centre for film and television, and they have extensive resources. These include international books and periodicals, newspaper clippings and scripts. The BFI Production Board helps finance British films: these films have included such productions as *Ascendency* and *The Draughtsman's Contract*. The National Film Theatre, whose aim is to screen the best of international cinema, has frequent lectures and film series. BFI also publishes a number of magazines and newsletters. There are several types of membership available, and for more information contact the membership secretary.

British Film and Television Producers Association (BFTPA)
Paramount House, 162 Wardour Street, London W1; 01-437 7700
The BFTPA, an amalgamation of the British Film Producers Association and the Federation of British Film-makers, represents the interests of the production side of the

industry. Members include major production companies, studios and independent producers. It is an employer's organisation and industrial relations are an important part of its activities. All producers of cinema and television films may become members. Among its services is an overseas committee to represent British productions abroad (particularly at film festivals) and a joint Industrial Relations Service with the Independent Programme Producers Association.

British Kinematograph, Sound and Television Society (BKSTS)

110-12 Vernon Place, Victoria House, London WC1B; 4DJ; 01-242 8400

The Society was formed by British technicians in 1931 to keep in touch with major technological developments. It holds regular meetings where new equipment is demonstrated. It publishes a monthly journal with technical articles and reviews as well as a series of technical manuals. There are three membership grades, including student membership. You must be over 16 years of age and be employed as a trainee in film, sound or television, or be enrolled in a full-time film studies course.

Directors Guild of Great Britain

56 Whitfield Street, London W1; 01-580 9592

The Directors Guild was established in 1982 to represent the interests of film, television and theatre directors in Britain. You need to have a professional directing credit for membership. (It does not need to be a union film.) The Guild holds workshops on directing which are open only to members. It also publishes a quarterly magazine and has an information service. Fees are on a sliding scale based on yearly income, from £25 per year for those earning less than £5000 per year, to £100 for those earning over £10,000 per year.

Guild of British Camera Technicians

303-15 Cricklewood Broadway, London NW2; 01-450 3821

The Guild is a professional organisation whose membership includes mostly cameramen/women. It provides information on rates of pay and seeks to improve working conditions. It runs a number of lectures, often in conjunction with the BKSTS, which are occasionally open to non-members.

Guild of British Film Editors

Spurland End Road, Great Kingshill, High Wycombe, Buckinghamshire; 0494 712313

The Guild is a professional organisation whose aim is to see that film and sound editing are recognised as a creative and important part of film production. Membership is open to editors with three feature film credits or who have been employed in cutting films for three consecutive years. It provides seminars and workshops for members on subjects ranging from use of new technology, laboratory processes and use of video.

Independent Film-makers Association (IFA)

79 Wardour Street, London W1; 01-439 0460

The IFA was founded in 1974 to represent the views and interests of a wide variety of groups who work with or through film and video. It involves not only film-makers but critics, teachers, and distribution workers. It is concerned with the development of independent cinema and has been closely involved with Channel 4. The Association receives its funding from Channel 4 and the British Film Institute. As well as a central office, the IFA has a number of regional offices which welcome newcomers who are interested in films.

Liverpool: Open Eye Workshop, 90-2 Whitechapel,
   Liverpool L1 6EN; 051-709 9460
Sheffield: 34 Psalter Lane, Sheffield 11
York: Jean Stewart, Hogg Farm, Intake Lane, Dunnington,
   Yorkshire; 0904 489067
East: EAFCO, Cinema City, St Andrew's Street, Norwich
   NR2 4AD; 0603 22313
East Midlands: New Cinema Workshop, 24-32 Carlton
   Street, Nottingham NG1 1NN; 0602 582636/583489
North-West: 5 James Leigh Street, Manchester M60 1SX

South-East: Brighton Film and Video Workshop, Watts
   Building, Brighton Polytechnic, Moulscombe, Brighton
   BN2 4JG; 0273 693655 ext 2183
South-West: 1 Elm Tree, 4 St Margaret's Road, Torquay
Wales: Chapter Arts Centre, Market Road, Canton, Cardiff
   CF5 1QE; 0222 396061
West: 37-9 Jamaica Street, Bristol BS2 8JP.

Independent Programme Producers Association (IPPA)
3 Fitzroy Square, London W1; 01-388 1234
The Independent Programme Producers Association which
was established in 1980, primarily as a result of the establishment of Channel 4, has almost 300 members. IPPA is a
service organisation for independent producers and is
responsible for negotiations between BFTPA and
independent service organisations. It is recognised by
Channel 4 as a negotiating body for independent film-
makers, but it is not recognised by the unions.

   The IPPA holds seminars for members on a variety of
topics and has a bulletin and newsletter. It also publishes
special booklets on specific topics of interest. It functions
as a resource centre and information service and is designed
to protect and further the interests of independent producers.

   You can apply for membership if you have already
produced a film or have the firm intention of doing so.
IPPA has both independent and corporate membership
available, with individual membership costing £50 per year
and corporate membership costing £200 per year.

Unions

Federation of Film Unions (FFU)
155 Kennington Park Road, London SE11 4JU;
01-735 9068
The FFU represents all the unions involved in film
production: ACTT, NATTKE, Equity, Electrical Tele-
communication and Plumbing Union, Film Artists' Association, Musicians' Union and Writers' Guild of Great Britain.
   Among the largest and most relevant of these unions for

jobs in the film industry that FFU represents are:

Association of Cinematograph, Television and allied Technicians (ACTT)

2 Soho Square, London, W1V 6DD; 01-437 8506

The ACTT, founded in 1933, is the largest union in the film industry. It represents the interests of people employed in most technical and production jobs in film. It lobbies on behalf of the film industry and negotiates trade agreements on behalf of its members. To become a member — virtually essential for anyone working in the film industry on the technical or production side (except producers) — you must have the offer of an ACTT-graded job which has been advertised within the Union's unemployment bureau. However, people with initiative will often find other ways in (like making themselves essential for a production so they *have* to be given a ticket). ACTT operates an employment register giving details of vacancies, which is published weekly; publishes a monthly magazine, *Film and TV Technician*; offers legal services to its members; and — pessimists will be glad to know — operates a funeral and benevolent fund. Membership subscription is 1 per cent of gross earnings excluding overtime.

Electrical Electronic Telecommunications and Plumbing Union

Hayes Court, West Common Road, Bromley BR2 7AU; 01-462 7755

A specialist union for lighting technicians.

Film Artists Union (FAA)

61 Marloes Road, London W8 6LF; 01-937 4567/8

The FAA represents extras, doubles and stand-ins. By agreement with the BFTPA all crowd scenes within 56 miles of Charing Cross must use FAA members.

Guild of British Camera Technicians

303-15 Cricklewood Broadway, London NW2; 01-450 3821

The Guild of British Camera Technicians specialises in camera technicians, many of whom, however, are members of ACTT.

National Association of Theatrical, Television and Kine Employees (NATTKE)
155 Kennington Park Road, London SE11; 01-735 9068
Formed in 1890 as a union for backstage theatre workers, it now has a virtual closed shop for clerical, secretarial, make-up, wardrobe, projection and cashier workers in the film industry.

Women's Organisations

In addition to these unions are a number of women's organisations and pressure groups whose aim is specifically to promote women in the industry and to combat any discrimination against them. Of these the major ones are:

Women's Broadcasting and Film Lobby
46 Warwick Avenue, London W9 2PU; 01-286 6027

Women in Entertainment
7 Thorpe Close, London W10; 01-969 2292

Women in Media
c/o Alison Hogan, 161 Hammersmith Grove, London W6; 01-286 1146

Women's Media Action Group
c/o Hungerford House, Victoria Embankment, London WC2
Publishes a bi-monthly bulletin, costing £2.40 per year.

Women's Research and Resources Centre
190 Upper Street, London N1; 01-359 5773
Includes a feminist film library, open 11 am to 5.30 pm Mondays to Saturdays.

Production Companies

'Right now it's only a notion, but I think I can get money to make it into a concept,' says the man at the Hollywood party in *Annie Hall*, 'and later turn it into an idea.' You cannot make a film without a concept, you cannot turn an idea into film without money, and you cannot get money without a production company. Production companies have other benefits to offer as well. Whether or not you have been to film school, a production company will often give you your first job. It may be a very menial job but it is a job in the film industry all the same, and will help you to build contacts for better things in the future. It is impossible to list all the production companies in Britain, but here are just a few of the larger and more dynamic ones. Some of them raise their own money for productions, others go into co-productions (often with Channel 4), while others still receive backing from distributors and subsidiaries.

Allied Stars
Pinewood Studios, Pinewood Road, Iver Heath, Buckinghamshire; 0753 651700
Partially Arab-financed, backed *Breaking Glass* (1979) and *Chariots of Fire* (1980).

Brent Walker
9 Chesterfield Street, London W1; 01-491 4430
Backed *Loophole* (1977) and *Return of the Soldier* (1981).

Columbia Pictures
19-23 Wells Street, London W1; 01-580 2090
French and US linked, backed Peter Yates's *Krull* (1983).

Goldcrest Films
131 Holland Park Avenue, London W11; 01-937 8022
One of the most dynamic and adventurous production companies in Britain today, a subsidiary of the Pearson Longman Group, backed by City finance; features include *Gandhi* (1981) and *Local Hero* (1982).

Handmade Films
26 Cadogan Square, London SW1; 01-584 8345
Backed by ex-Beatle George Harrison and the Monty Python team; produced *Scrubbers*, *Privates on Parade* and *The Missionary* in 1982.

Island Pictures
22 St Peter's Square, London W6 9NW; 01-741 1511
A subsidiary of the record company. Its first excursion into

film was Jimmy Cliff's *The Harder They Come* (1971), and had grown up specialising in video films of its recording artists; recently it has backed *Countryman* (1981) and *Accident* (1982).

J and M Sales
9 Clifford Street, London W1; 01-734 2181
Mainly a distributor which sells and pre-sells independent productions to independent distributors handling, amongst others, Euan Lloyd's *Who Dares Wins*.

The Ladd Company
44 Earlham Street, London WC2; 01-836 7673
A subsidiary of Warner Bros, whose feature films include *Blade Runner* (1981).

MGM-UA
11 Hamilton Place, London W1; 01-741 9041
One of the largest and most active production companies in Britain, making *The Hunger*, *Eureka* and *Octopussy* in 1982.

Paramount Pictures
162 Wardour Street, London W1; 01-437 7700
Owned by Gulf and Western, made Roger Christian's *Dollar Bottom* (which won him an Oscar) and *The Sender*.

Producers' Sales Organisation
120 Pall Mall, London SW1; 01-839 3293
An international sales organisation selling the work of independent producers to independent distributors.

Rank Films Distributors
127 Wardour Street, London W1V 4AD; 01-437 9020
Made *Heat and Dust* and *Boys in Blue* in 1982.

Rediffusion Films Ltd
PO Box 451, Carlton House, Lower Regent Street, London SW1Y 4LS; 01-930 0221
Backed Michael Radford's *Another Time — Another Place*; now concentrates on co-productions with Channel 4.

Thorn EMI Films
142 Wardour Street, London W1 4AE; 01-437 0444
Backed *Britannia Hospital* (1981).

Twentieth Century-Fox
30 Soho Square, London W1V 6AP; 01-437 7766
A large US major, which made *Alien* and *Star Wars*, and also co-financed *Chariots of Fire* and *The Final Conflict* (with Allied Stars).

Universal Pictures
170 Piccadilly, London W1V 9FH; 01-629 7211
A US major whose UK-backed productions include *Pirates of Penzance* (1981) and *Monty Python — The Meaning of Life* (1982).

Virgin Films
8 Poland Street, London W1; 01-221 7535
One of the newest British production companies and an offshoot of the record company, Virgin Films is regarded as having the potential of being one of the most adventurous production companies in the country.

Warner Brothers
Pinewood Studios, Iver Heath, Buckinghamshire SL0 0NH; 0753 654545
Produced *Superman III*, *Never Say Never Again* and *Greystoke*.

Michael White
13 Duke Street, London SW1Y 6DB; 01-839 3771
Mainly a theatrical impresario, but recently moved into low-budget films, including *Moonlighting* (1983).

Publications

Following is a selection of film and television publications including journals, magazines, newspapers and books. Many can be obtained direct from the organisation involved, or purchased from specialist film bookstores or newsagents around Soho. A number can also be studied in the BFI Library. Few of the publications have job advertisements, but they will help keep you informed on the activities within the industry, and help familiarise you with names of companies and productions.

Journals

Afterimage: 1 Birnham Road, London N4
Somewhat highbrow and theoretical with each issue specialising on one particular genre or area of film.

AIP and Co: Association of Independent Producers, 17 Pulteney Street, London W1; 01-734 1581
First rate journal of AIP, with excellent features on film. Can be purchased from large newsagents, bookshops specialising in film and from the AIP offices. Published monthly.

BFI News: 127 Charing Cross, London WC2; 01-437 4355
BFI journal for members, published bi-monthly, with good listing.

Broadcast: 32-4 Great Marlborough Street, London W1; 01-439 9756/734 4801
Although specialising in television, it has a wide range of features on the film and video industry. Published weekly.

Bulletin of the Royal Television Society: Tavistock House East, Tavistock Square, London WC1; 01-387 1970
RTS bulletin with events and television industry news items. Since the arrival of Channel 4 it now contains articles and news on the film industry, particularly where there is a film production company co-production with Channel 4. Published monthly.

The Business: 56 Grosvenor Street, London W1; 01-499 9933
Publication aimed at professionals in the film industry, including producers, exhibitors and distributors. Published monthly.

Film: British Federation of Film Societies, BFI, 81 Dean Street, London W1V 6AA; 01-437 4355
Information about non-commercial aspects of film, published monthly.

Film and Filming: 445 Brighton Road, South Croydon, Surrey CR2 6EU; 01-660 3602
Reviews, features and interviews on films, published monthly.

Film Review: EMI Cinemas Ltd, Old Court House, Old Court Place, London W8; 01-937 4260
Publishes information about all English-language films on release and in production. Published monthly.

Film and Television Technician: ACTT, 2 Soho Square, London W1; 01-437 8506
House journal for ACTT members.

Framework: English and American Studies, University of East Anglia, Norwich NR4 7TS; 0603 56161
Very intellectual magazine on film theory and aesthetics. Keep a dictionary handy when you try to read it. Published irregularly.

The Hollywood Reporter: 6715 Sunset Boulevard, Hollywood, California 90028, USA
American trade paper available in large or specialist newsagents in London. Published daily.

Monthly Film Bulletin: BFI, 81 Dean Street, London W1V 6AA; 01-437 4355
Interviews and features, plus credits and synopses of all UK releases.

Screen Digest: 37 Gower Street, London WC1E 6HH; 01-580 2842
A digest of film industry news, with special features and pull-outs on specific areas, such as laws, sales, etc. Published monthly.

Screen International: 6-7 Chapel Street, London W1; 01-734 9452
Cinema industry magazine with news of productions and forthcoming productions. Published weekly.

Sight and Sound: BFI, 81 Dean Street, London W1V 6AA; 01-437 4355
Most established of film magazines in Britain, now 52

years old, as much Establishment as established, but worth reading. Published quarterly.

Books and Reference Books

Most of these are available at the BFI Library.

American Film Institute Guide to College Courses in Film and Television: Book Order Department, Peterson's Guide, Department 7591, PO Box 978, Edison, New Jersey 08817, USA.
Gives full listings of film schools and workshops in the USA and Canada.

A Biographical Dictionary of the Cinema: by David Thompson, Secker and Warburg, London, 1975, revised 1980.
A 'Who's Who' of directors, producers and actors. 'Personal, opinionated and obsessive', according to its author.

BFI Film and Television Yearbook: British Film Institute, 1983.
This is a vital book. Contains excellent listings of colleges, workshops, organisations, hire facilities and production companies, as well as good end-of-year articles on the state of British films.

British Cinema Now: edited by Martin Auty, British Film Institute.
First-rate collection of essays on the current state of the British film industry.

Cinema. A Critical Dictionary: edited by Richard Roud, Secker and Warburg, London, 1980.
Two volumes, containing both biographical and critical entries.

A Critical History of the British Cinema: by Roy Armes, Secker and Warburg, London, 1979.
Good history of the British cinema, though its between-the-lines implication that anyone making good films should be left-wing can be mildly irritating.

The Film Business: by Ernest Betts, George Allen and Unwin, London, 1973.
Another good history of the British cinema, strong on the economic and business side, and with an excellent essay by John Grierson on the British documentary movement.

The Filmgoer's Companion: by Leslie Halliwell, Hart-Davies, 1974.
Already the classic reference book on films, it is a biographical dictionary, with additional sections on subjects and fictitious characters.

Filmmaker's Handbook: by Steve Bernstein, Focal Press, Butterworths, to be published March 1985.
The same Steve Bernstein who heads Crosswind and has a reputation as one of the best teachers of film in Britain. His book, which will be an attempt to pass on some of his knowledge, should be very good.

Film Review 1982-83: edited by Maurice Speed, W H Allen, London, 1983.
A good yearly collection of film reviews and articles on the cinema.

The Guinness Book of Film Facts and Feats: by Patrick Robertson, Guinness Superlatives Ltd, 1980.
An illustrated compendium of everything you don't really need to know about the cinema, but which is fascinating all the same.

Halliwell's Film Guide: by Leslie Halliwell, Granada, London, 1981.
Another great Halliwell tome, with over 10,000 entries, plus credits and critical opinions.

Independent Film Production Handbook: edited by James Park and Sue Eatwell, AIP, 1983.
AIP's yearly looseleaf guide to independent directors; a mine of useful information.

The International Encyclopaedia of Film: edited by Roger Manvell and others, Michael Joseph, London, 1972.

In addition to individual entries it contains general articles on both the creative and technical developments in British cinema.

The International Film Encyclopaedia: by Ephraim Katz, Macmillan, London, 1980.
Over 7000 entries, biographical, technical and critical.

International Film Guide 1983: edited by Peter Cowie, Tantivy Press, 1983.
Features and information on film books, guides, magazines, schools, workshops and festivals.

International Film and TV Yearbook 1982-83: edited by Peter Noble, Screen International Publications, 1983.
Yearly run-down on world cinema with articles, features and information; well-recommended.

Opportunities in Film: by Jan Bone, VGM Career Horizons, 1983.
A useful how-to-get-a-job book for anyone wanting to make a career in film-making in the USA.

The Oxford Companion to Film: edited by Liz-Ann Bawden, Oxford University Press, 1976.
Over 3000 entries on all aspects of film, in Britain and abroad.

Production 82-83: edited by Patricia Williams, Broadcast, 1983.
Good guide to Britain's film, video and TV production companies, with full listings.

Reel Facts: edited by Cobbett Steinberg, Penguin, 1981.
A sort of plain-clothes *Guinness Book of Records*, full of the best of everything, but also contains useful information on awards, festivals and studios.

The World Encyclopaedia of the Film: edited by John M Smith and Tim Cawkwell, Studio Vista, 1972.
Biographical entries and a film index with over 22,000 entries.

33/125

ISA   58G 70111

The. ~~Guar~~